50 Broadway Shows / 50 Broadway Songs

ISBN 978-0-7935-0759-7

HAL•LEONARD®
CORPORATION
7777 W. BLUEMOUND RD. P.O. BOX 13819 MILWAUKEE, WI 53213

Visit Hal Leonard Online at
www.halleonard.com

ANY DREAM WILL DO

from JOSEPH AND THE AMAZING TECHNICOLOR® DREAMCOAT

Music by ANDREW LLOYD WEBBER
Lyrics by TIM RICE

3

way   some - one was weep - ing,

but the world was sleep - ing,   an - y dream will

do.   I wore my coat

CHOIR:

I wore my

break - ing, and the world was wak - ing,

ah, _____ ah, ____

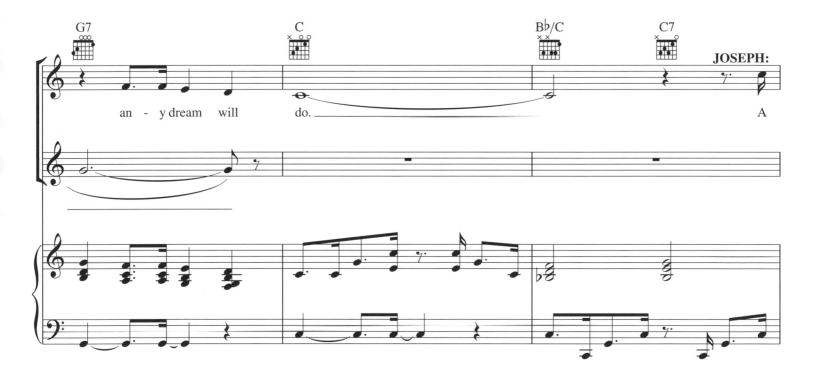

an - y dream will do. _____ A

JOSEPH:

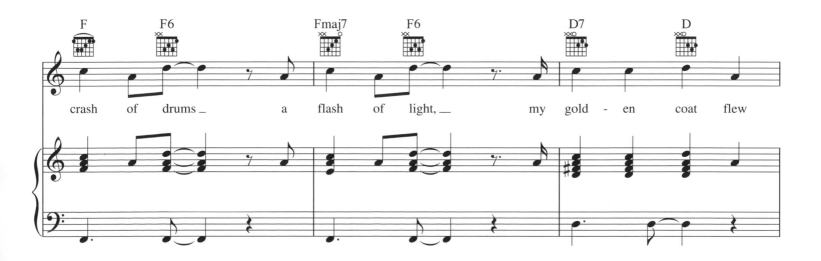

crash of drums _ a flash of light, _ my gold - en coat flew

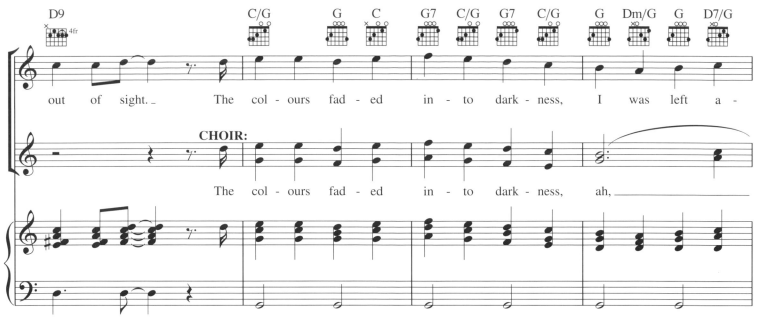

out of sight. The col-ours fad-ed in-to dark-ness, I was left a-

CHOIR:

The col-ours fad-ed in-to dark-ness, ah,

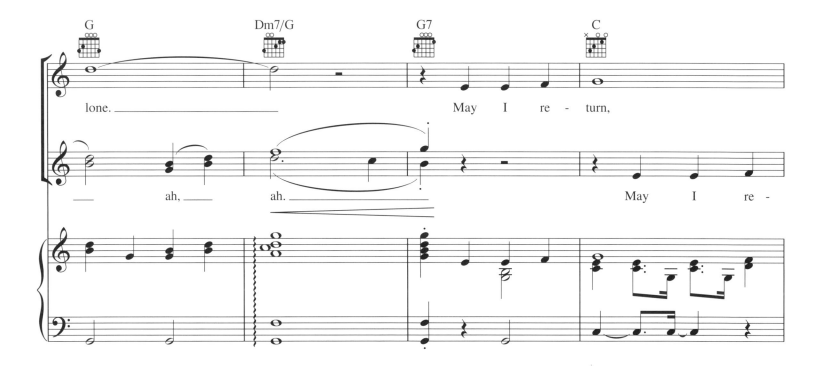

lone. May I re-turn,

ah, ah.

May I re-

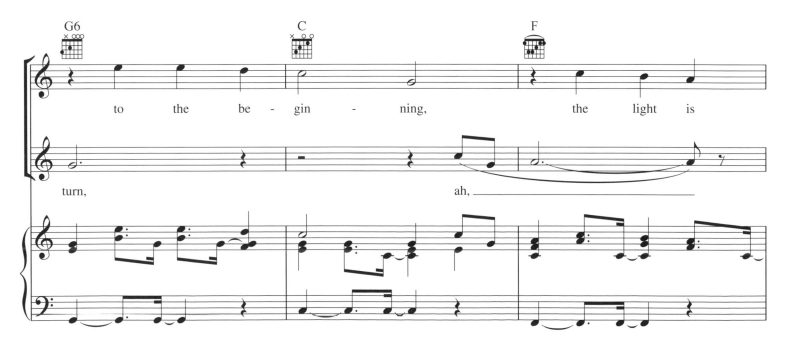

to the be-gin-ning, the light is

turn, ah,

dim - ming   and the dream is too,

ah. _____

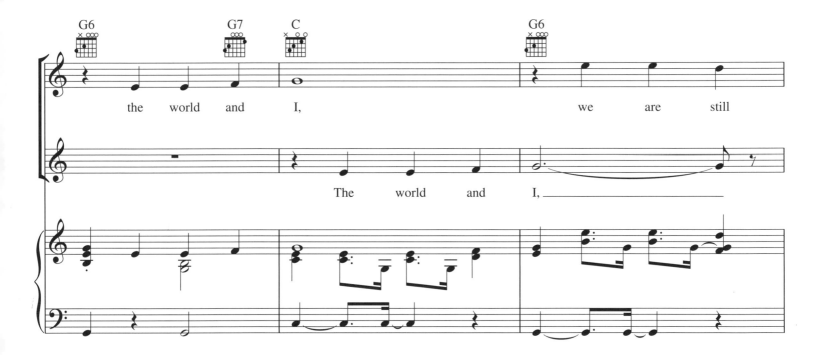

the world and I,   we are still

The world and I, _____

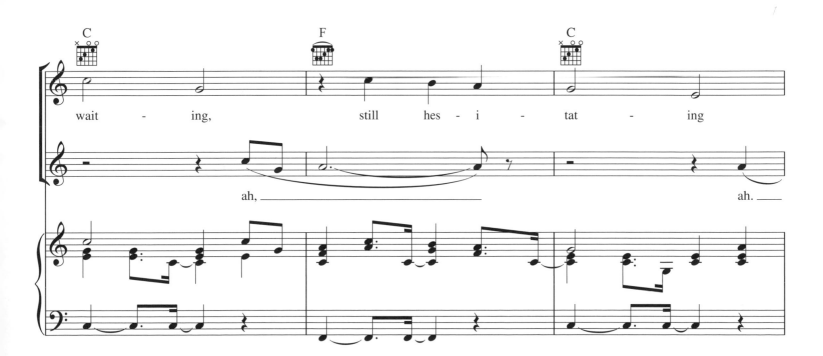

wait - ing,   still hes - i - tat - ing

ah, _____   ah. ___

AS IF WE NEVER SAID GOODBYE

from SUNSET BOULEVARD

Music by ANDREW LLOYD WEBBER
Lyrics by DON BLACK and CHRISTOPHER HAMPTON,
with contributions by AMY POWERS

Feel the ear-ly morn-ing mad - ness, _____ feel the

mag - ic in the mak - ing. _____ Why, ev - 'ry-thing's as if we

nev - er said good - bye. _____ I've

spent so man - y morn - ings, _____ just try - ing to re - sist you. _____

13

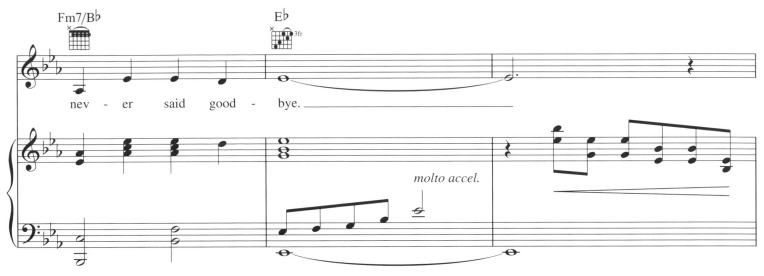

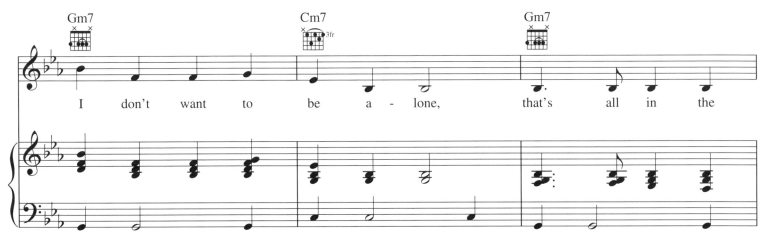

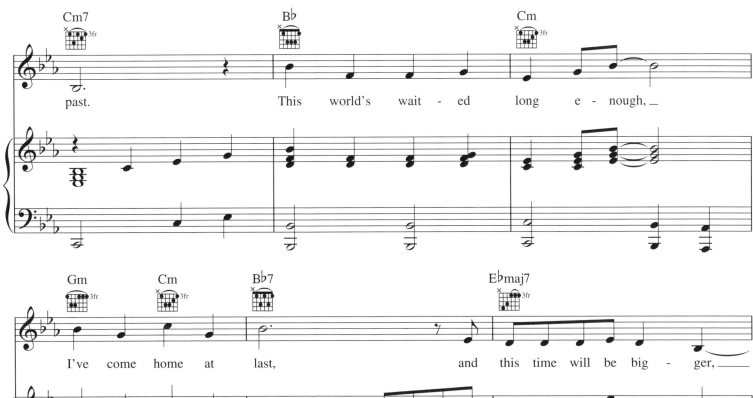

and bright - er than we knew it. ____ So watch me fly, ___ we all know I ___ can do it. ____ ___ Could I stop my hand from shak - ing? ____ Has there ev - er been a mo - ment ____ with so much to

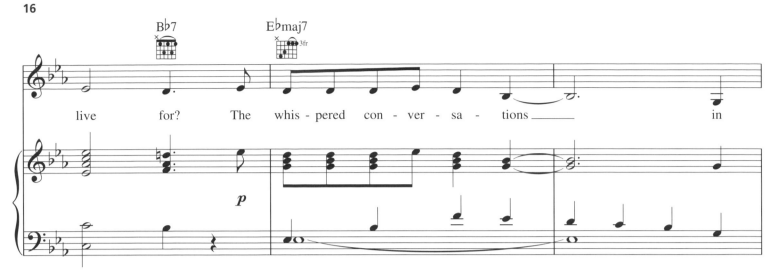

live for? The whis-pered con - ver - sa - tions _____ in

o - ver-crowd-ed hall - ways, _____ so much to say, not

just to - day, _ but al - ways. _____ We'll have

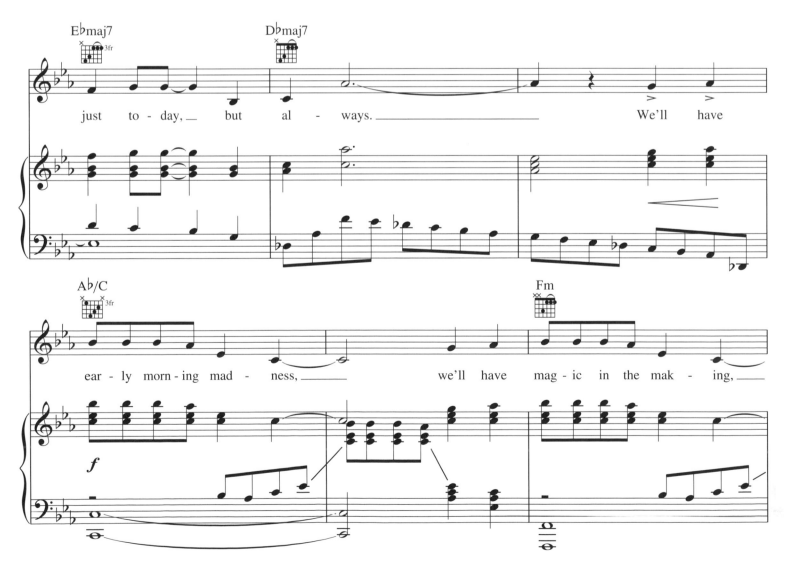

ear - ly morn-ing mad - ness, _____ we'll have mag - ic in the mak - ing, _____

AS LONG AS HE NEEDS ME

from the Broadway Musical OLIVER!

Words and Music by
LIONEL BART

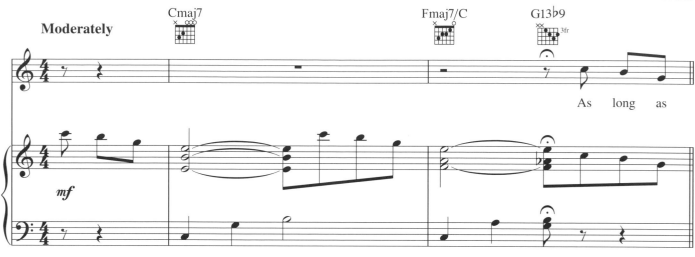

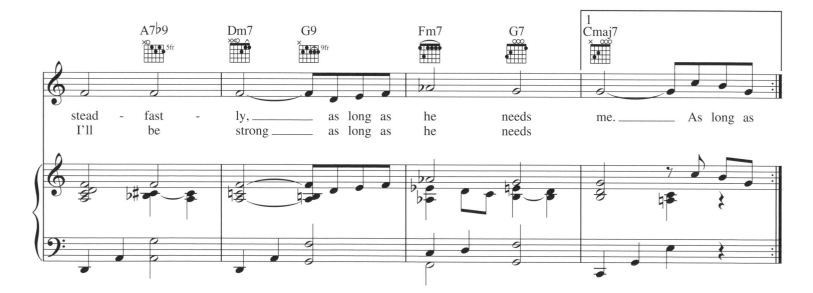

me._____ If you are lone - ly _____ then you will know _____ when some - one

needs you _____ you love them so. _____ I won't be - tray his

trust, _____ though peo - ple say I must._____ I've got to

stay true, just _____ as long as he needs me.

BEAUTY AND THE BEAST

from Walt Disney's BEAUTY AND THE BEAST: THE BROADWAY MUSICAL

Lyrics by HOWARD ASHMAN
Music by ALAN MENKEN

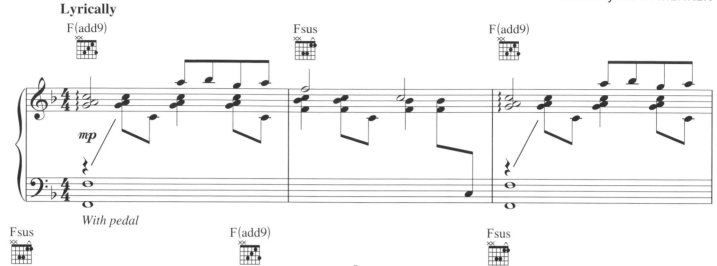

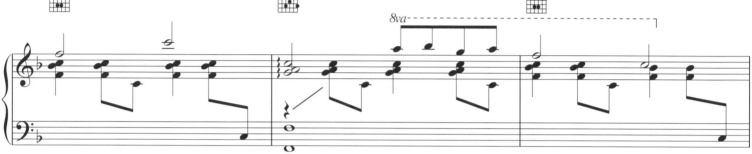

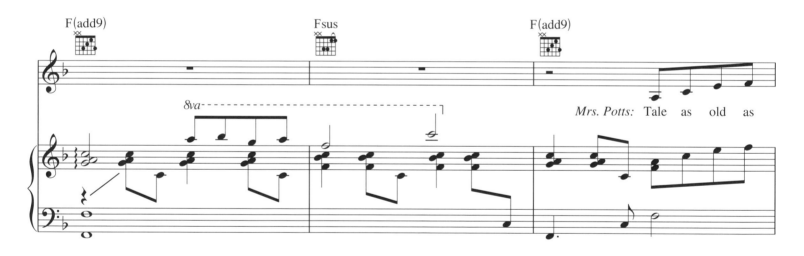

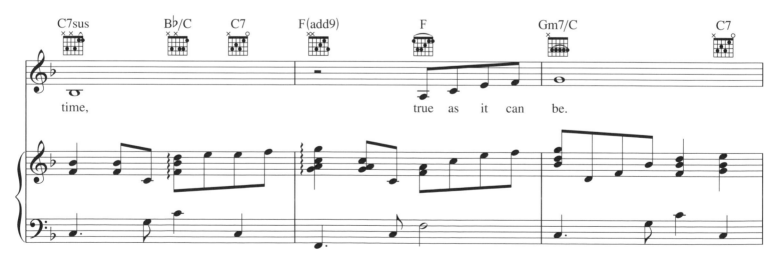

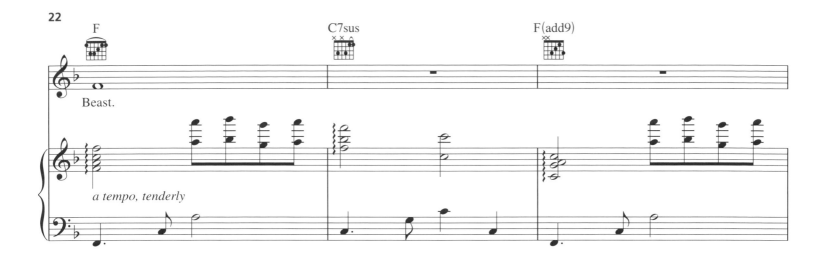

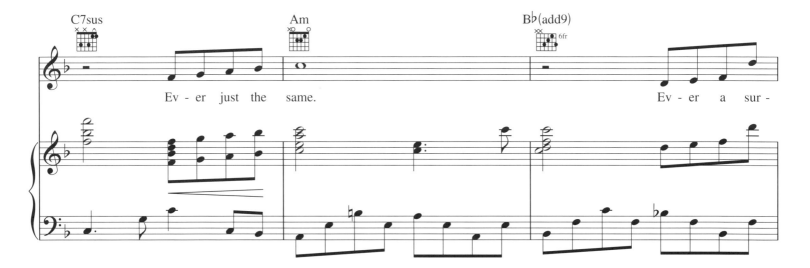

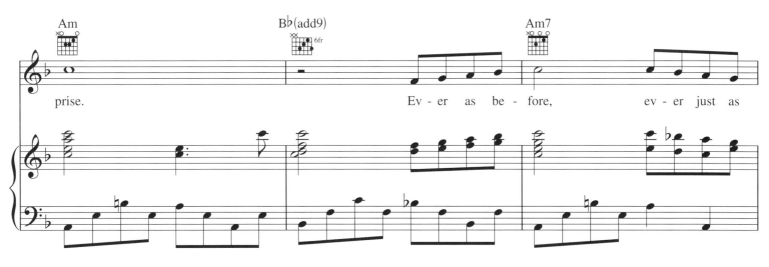

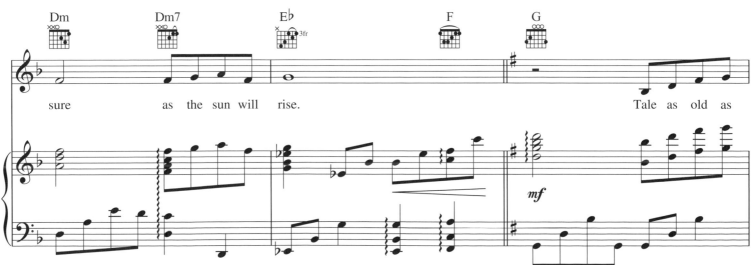

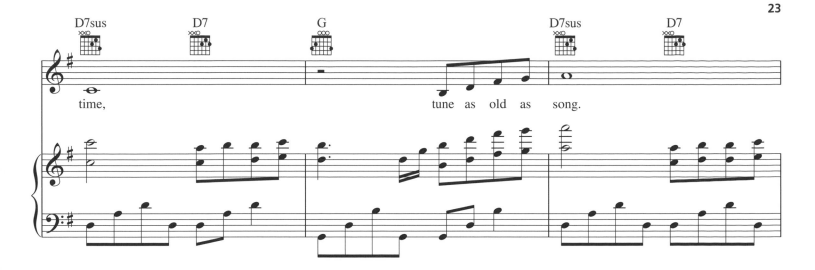

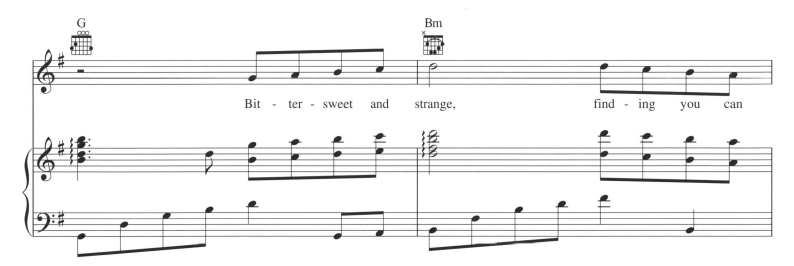

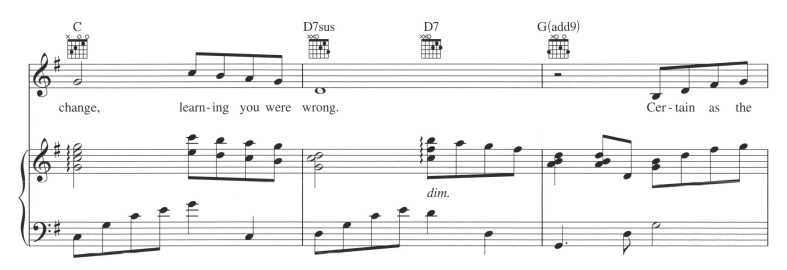

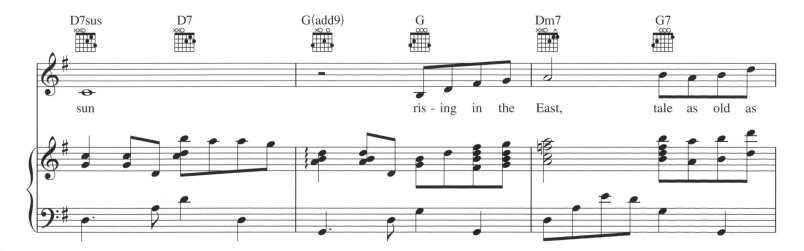

24

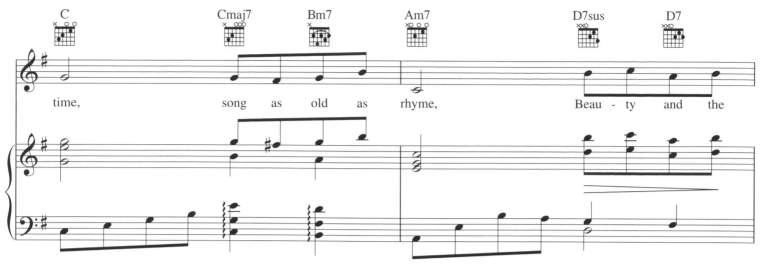

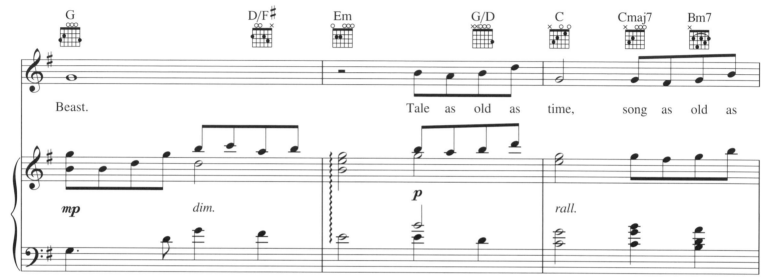

BEING ALIVE

from COMPANY

Words and Music by
STEPHEN SONDHEIM

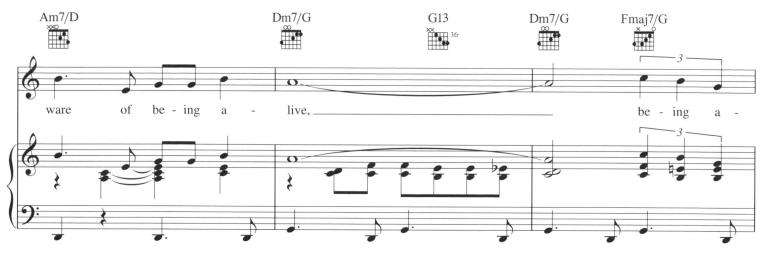

ware of be - ing a - live, _____ be - ing a -

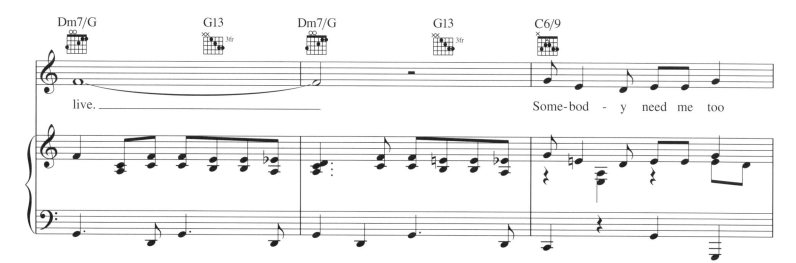

live. _____ Some-bod - y need me too

much, some - bod - y know me too well,

some - bod - y pull me up short, and put me through hell, and give me sup -

29

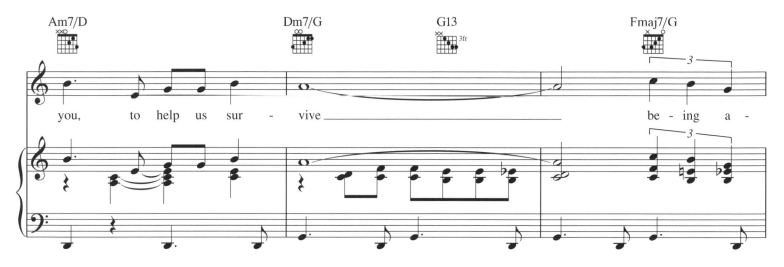

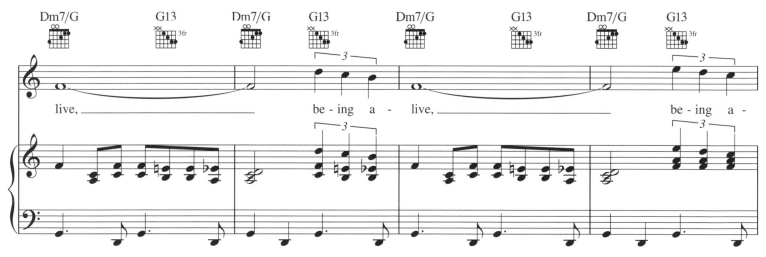

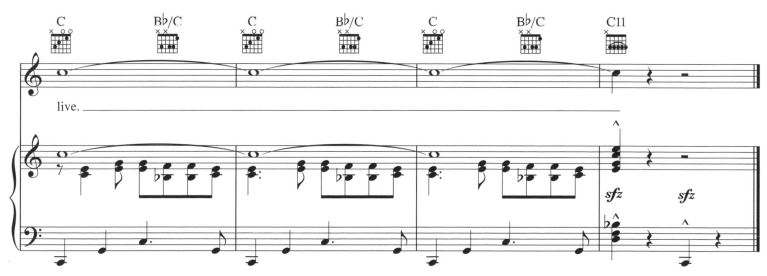

BEWITCHED
from PAL JOEY

Words by LORENZ HART
Music by RICHARD RODGERS

Moderately

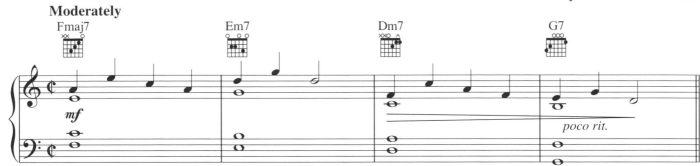

Not fast

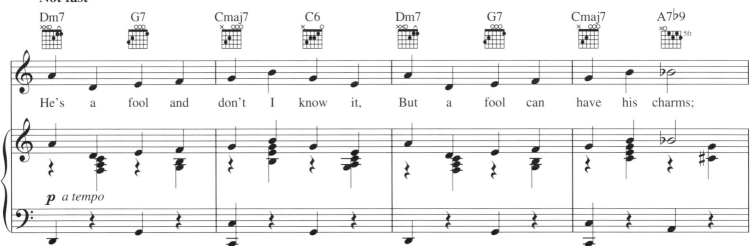

He's a fool and don't I know it, But a fool can have his charms;

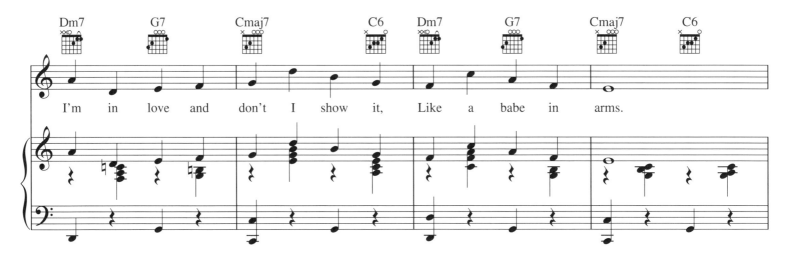

I'm in love and don't I show it, Like a babe in arms.

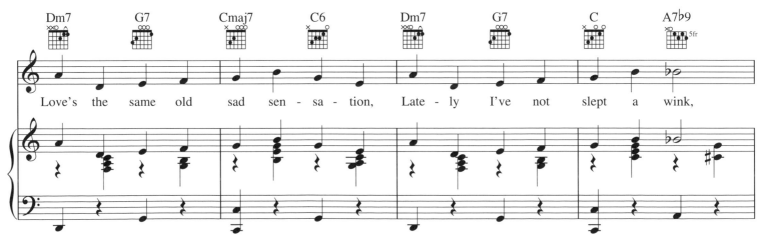

Love's the same old sad sen-sa-tion, Late-ly I've not slept a wink,

Since this half-pint im-i-ta-tion, Put me on the blink. I'm

Slowly

wild a-gain, be-guiled a-gain, a sim-per-ing, whim-per-ing

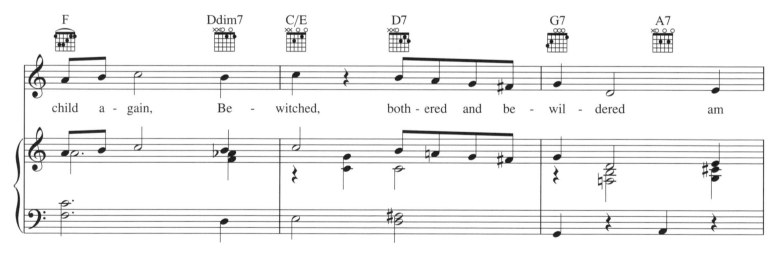

child a-gain, Be-witched, both-ered and be-wil-dered am

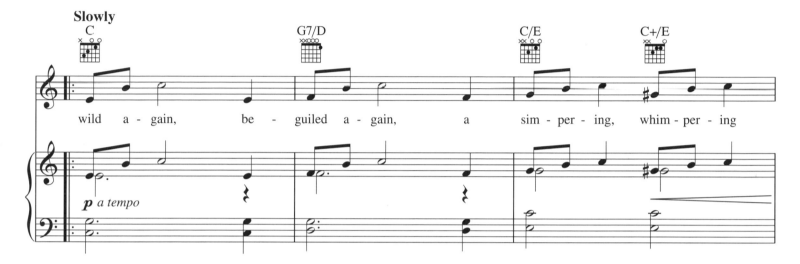

I. _____ Could-n't sleep, and would-n't sleep, When

love came and told me I should-n't sleep, Be - witched, both - ered and be -

wil - dered am I.

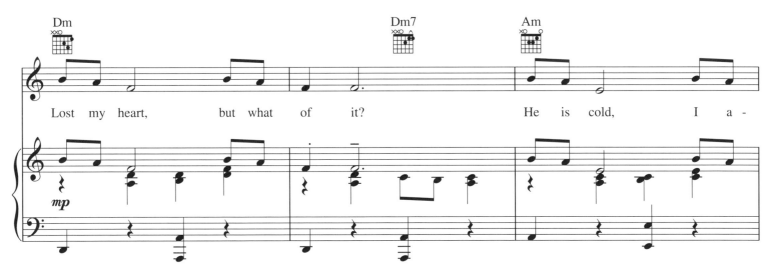

Lost my heart, but what of it? He is cold, I a -

gree, He can laugh, but I love it, Al - though the

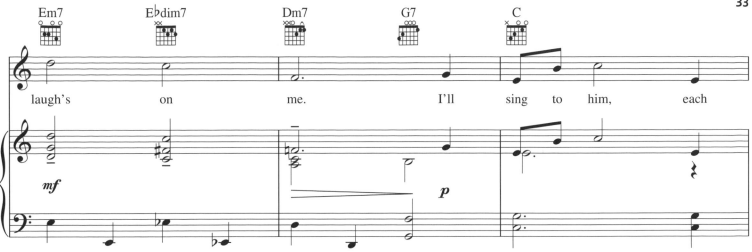

laugh's on me. I'll sing to him, each

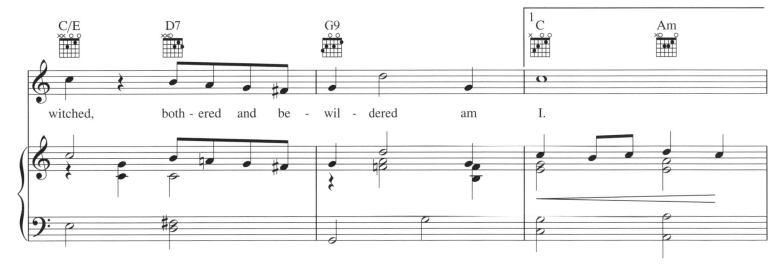

spring to him, And long for the day when I'll cling to him, Be -

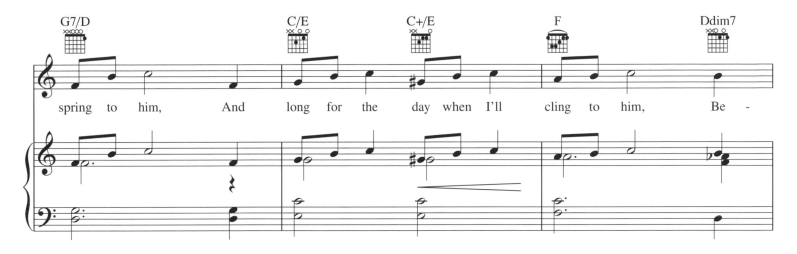

witched, both - ered and be - wil - dered am I.

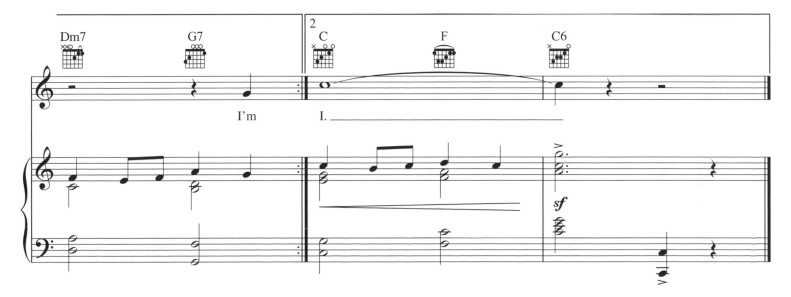

I'm I.

BIG SPENDER
from SWEET CHARITY

Music by CY COLEMAN
Lyrics by DOROTHY FIELDS

The min-ute you walked in the joint, I could see you were a man of dis-tinc-tion, a

real big spend-er! Good look-ing, so re-fined. _ Say,

would-n't you like to know what's go-ing on in my mind? _ So let me get right to the point,

35

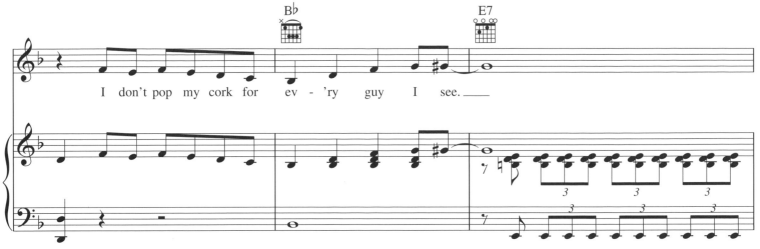

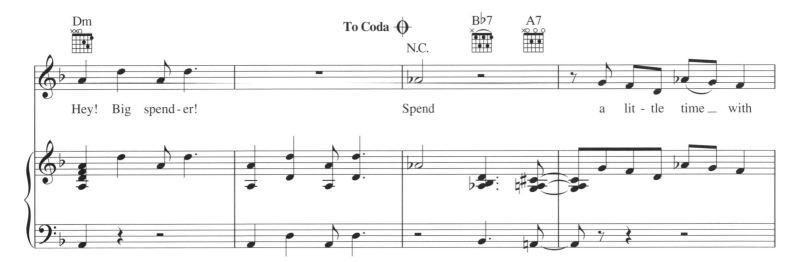

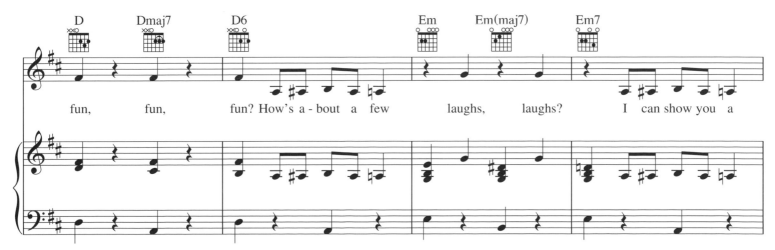

good time._____ Let me show you a good time._____ The min-ute you

Hey, big spend-er! Hey, big spend-er!

Spend _____ a lit-tle time_ with me. Spend a lit-tle time_ with

me. Spend a lit-tle time_ with me. _____

DAY BY DAY
from the Musical GODSPELL

Music by STEPHEN SCHWARTZ
Lyrics by RICHARD OF CHICHESTER (1197-1253)

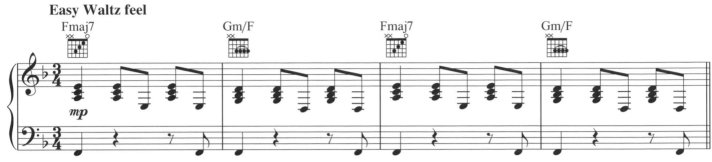

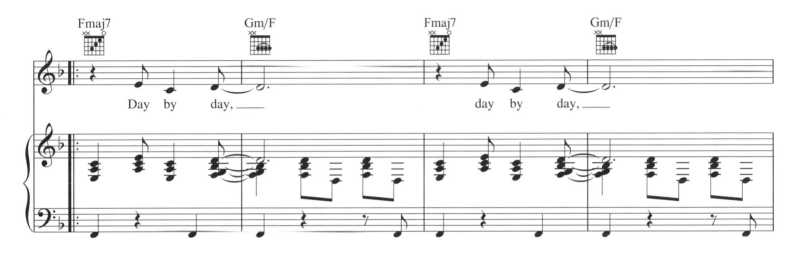

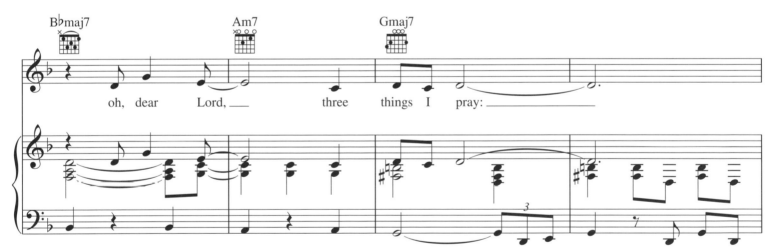

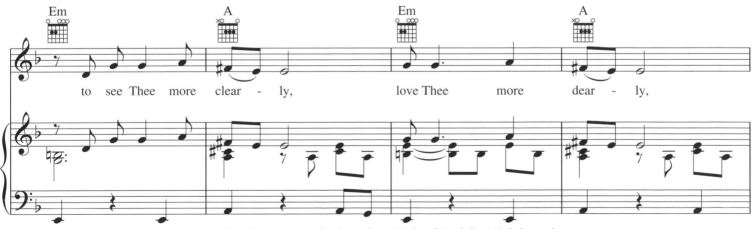

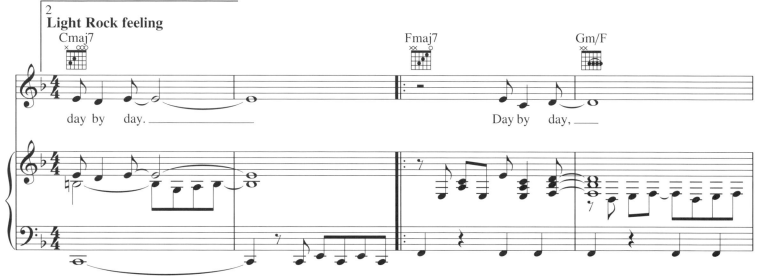

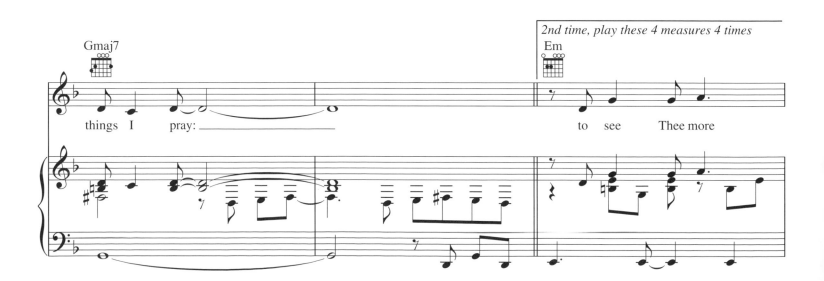

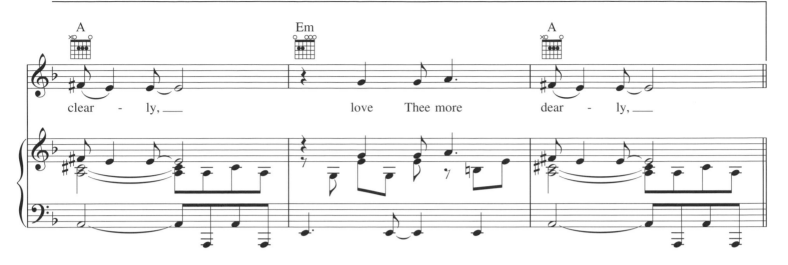

clear - ly, ___ love Thee more dear - ly, ___

fol - low Thee more near - ly, ___ day by day. ___

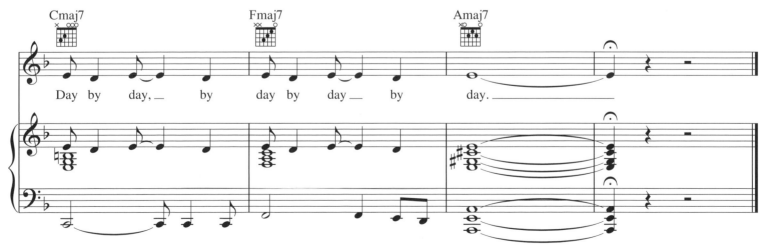

day by day.

Day by day, _ by day by day _ by day. ___

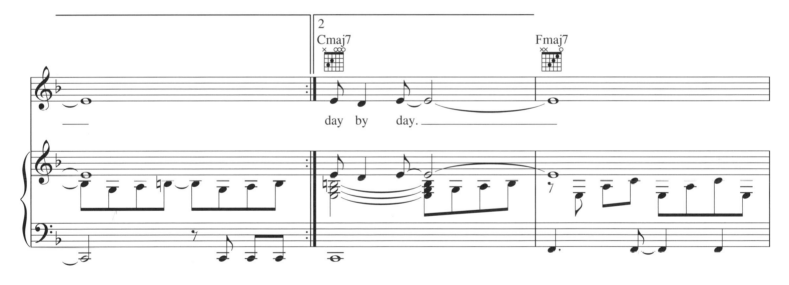

CABARET
from the Musical CABARET

Words by FRED EBB
Music by JOHN KANDER

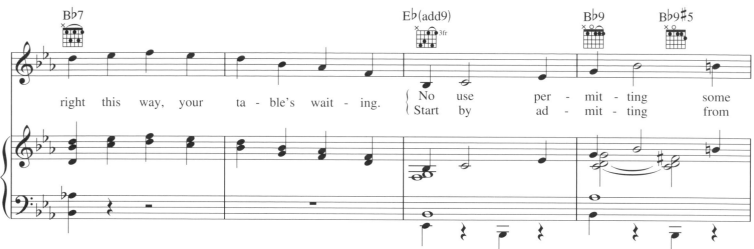

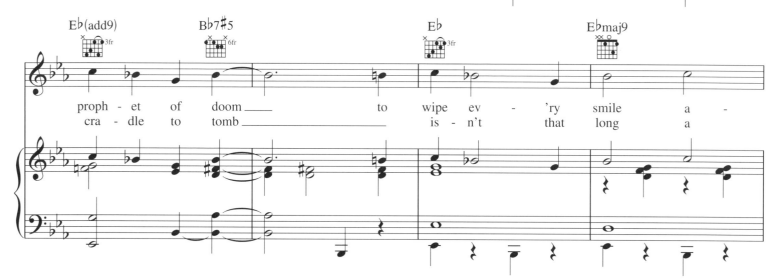

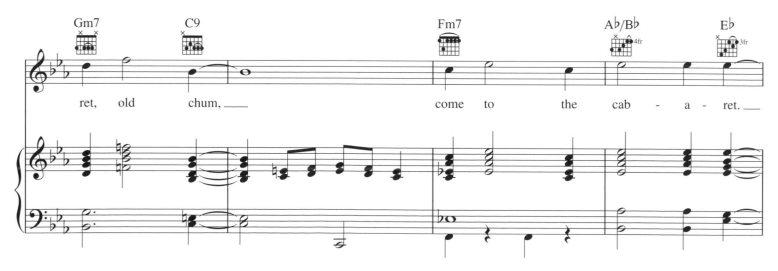

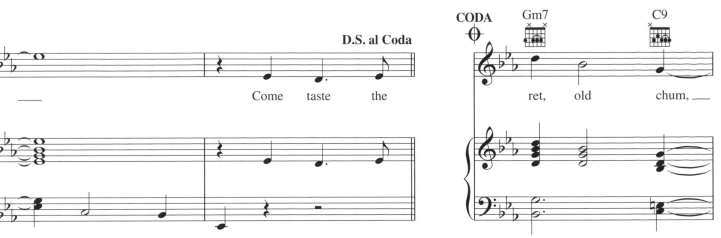

D.S. al Coda

CODA

Come taste the

ret, old chum, ___

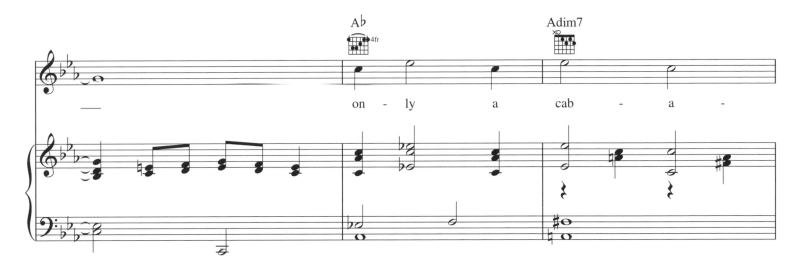

on - ly a cab - a -

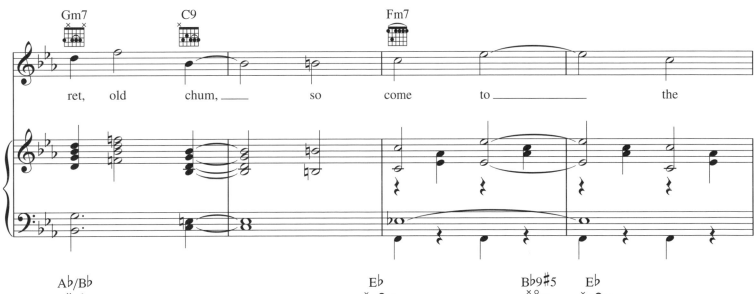

ret, old chum, ___ so come to ___ the

cab - a - ret. ___

DON'T CRY FOR ME ARGENTINA

from EVITA

Words by TIM RICE
Music by ANDREW LLOYD WEBBER

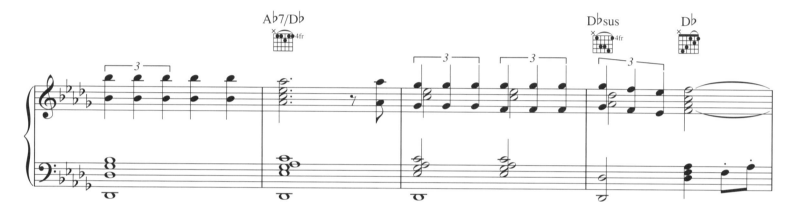

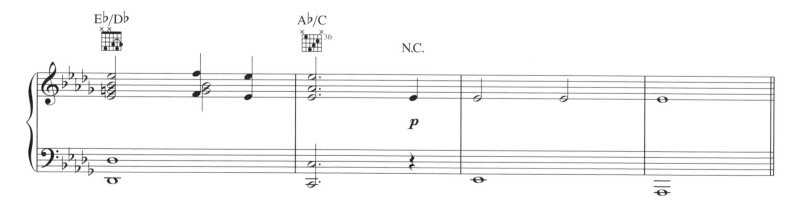

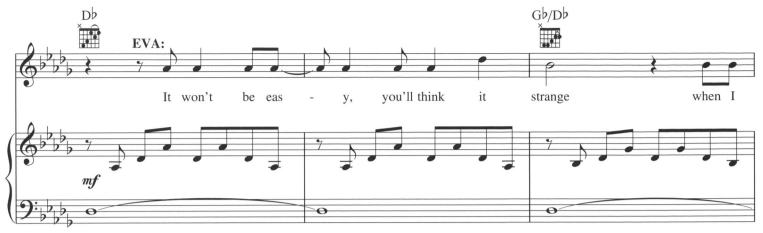

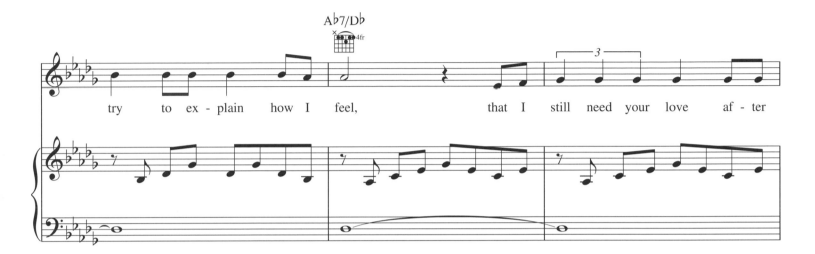

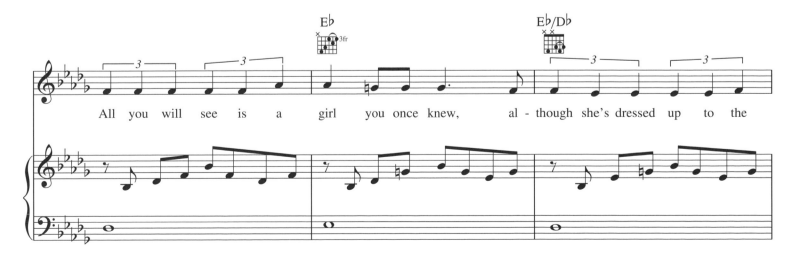

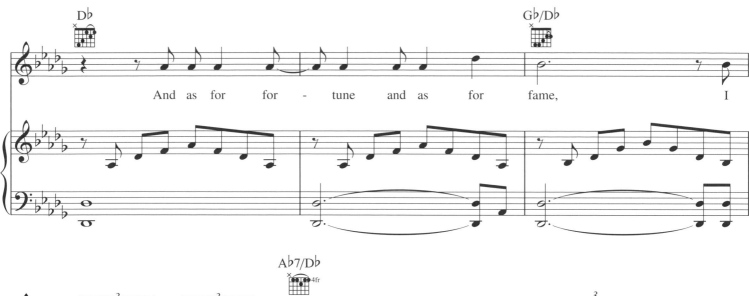

And as for for - tune and as for fame,   I

nev - er in - vit - ed them in,   though it seemed to the world __ they were

all I de - sired. _____ They are il - lu - sions, they're

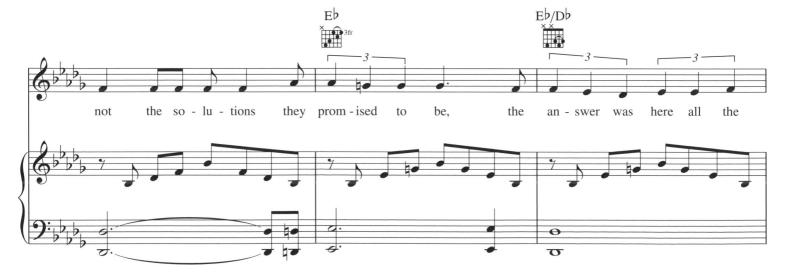

not the so - lu - tions they prom - ised to be,   the an - swer was here all the

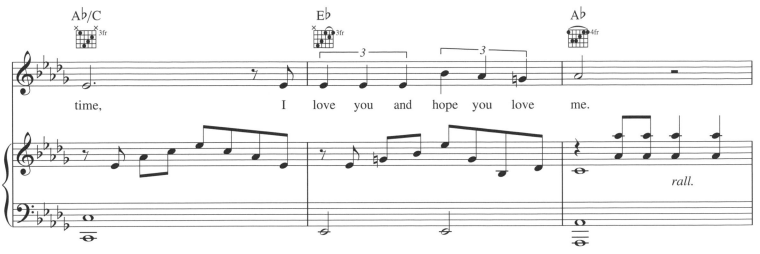

time,   I love you and hope you love me.

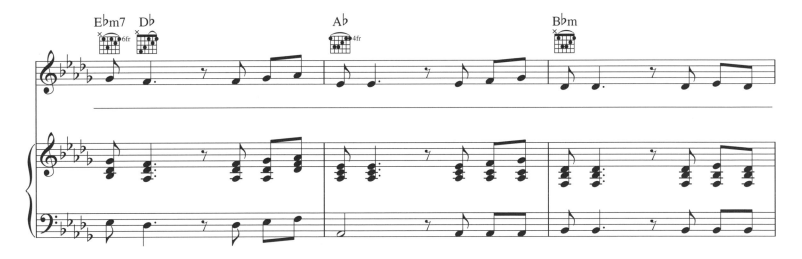

Don't cry for me Ar - gen - ti - na.   Mm

Don't cry for me Ar - gen -

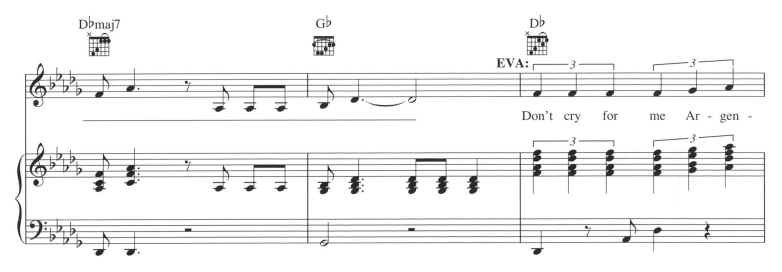

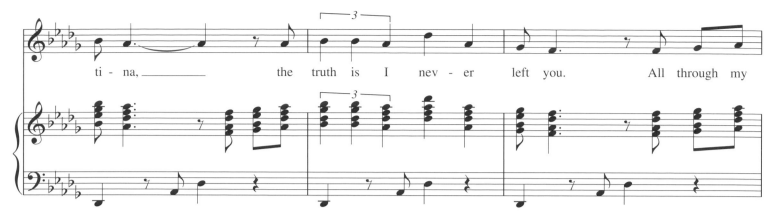

ti - na, _____ the truth is I nev - er left you. All through my

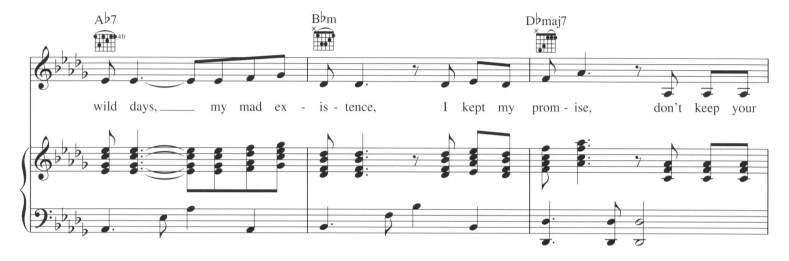

wild days, _____ my mad ex - is - tence, I kept my prom - ise, don't keep your

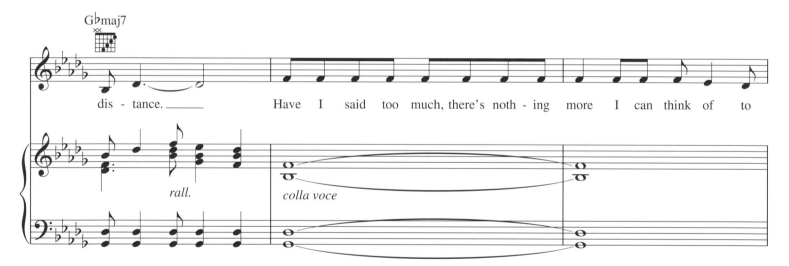

dis - tance. _____ Have I said too much, there's noth - ing more I can think of to

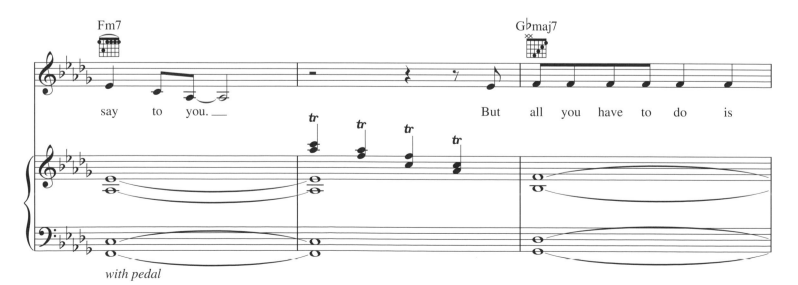

say to you. ___ But all you have to do is

with pedal

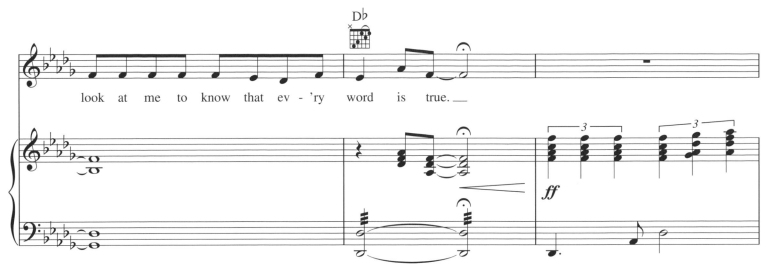

look at me to know that ev - 'ry word is true.

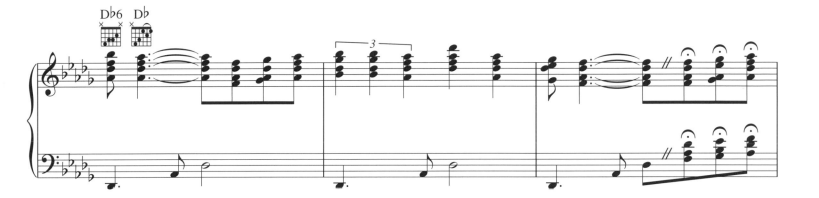

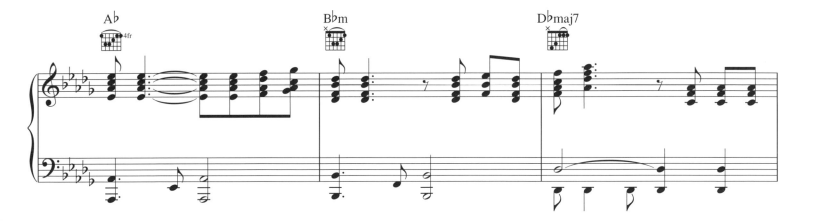

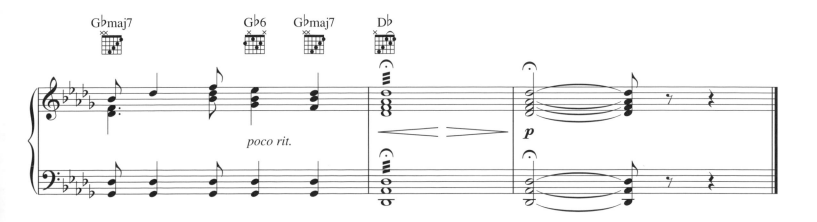

poco rit.

EVERYTHING'S COMING UP ROSES

from GYPSY

Words by STEPHEN SONDHEIM
Music by JULE STYNE

Briskly

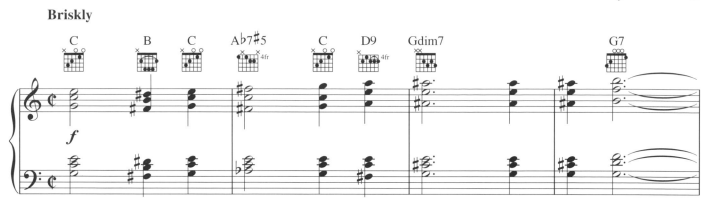

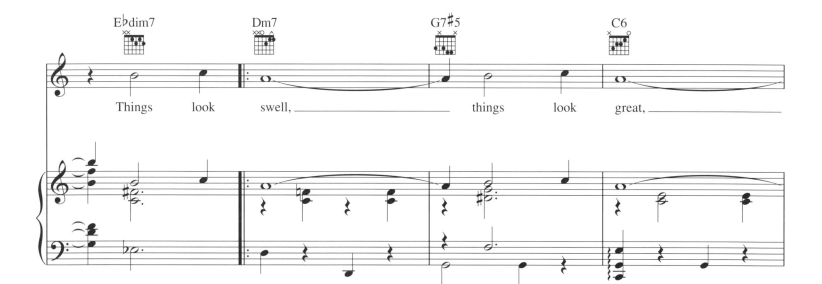

Things look swell, _____ things look great, _____

_____ gon - na have the whole world _____ on a plate. _____

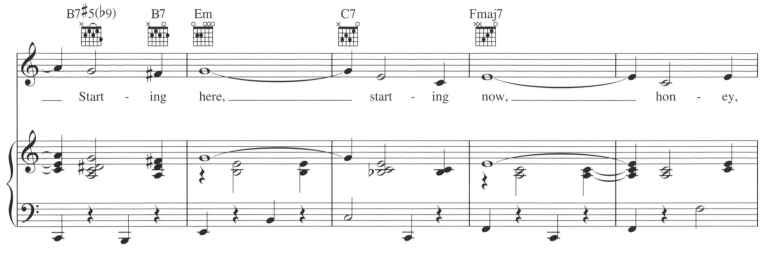

Starting here, starting now, honey,

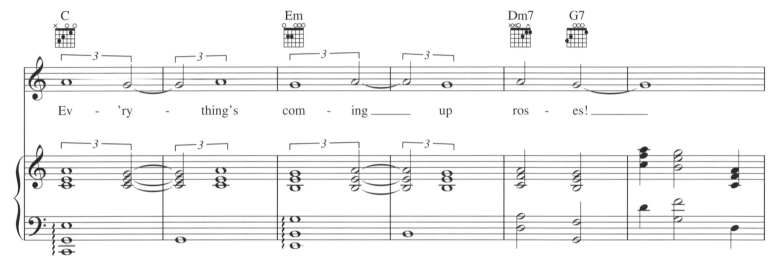

Ev - 'ry - thing's com - ing up ros - es!

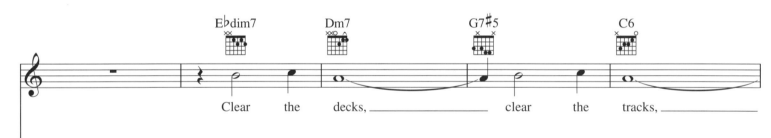

Clear the decks, clear the tracks,

we got noth - ing to do but re - lax.

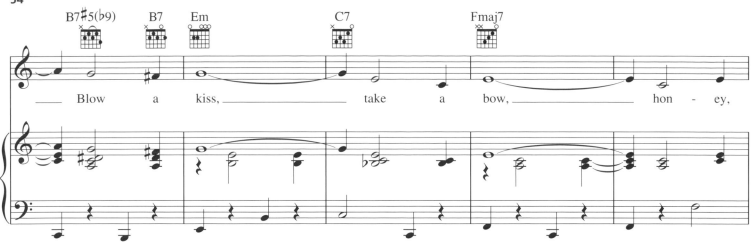

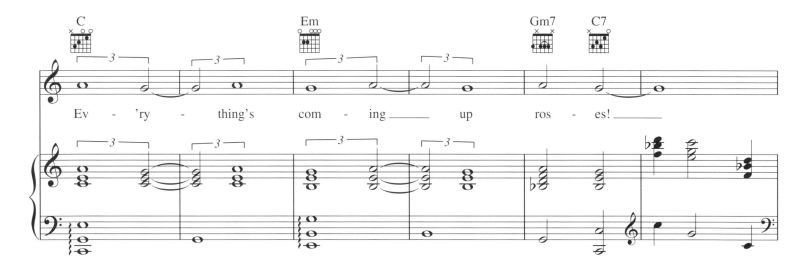

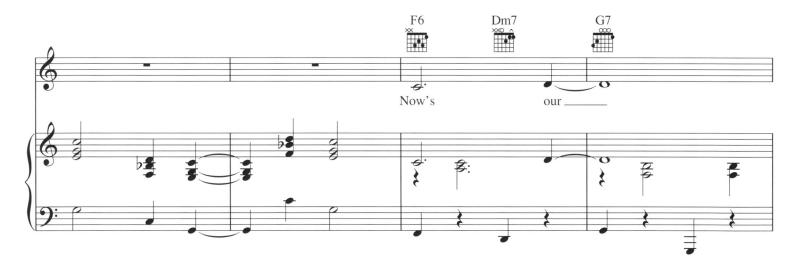

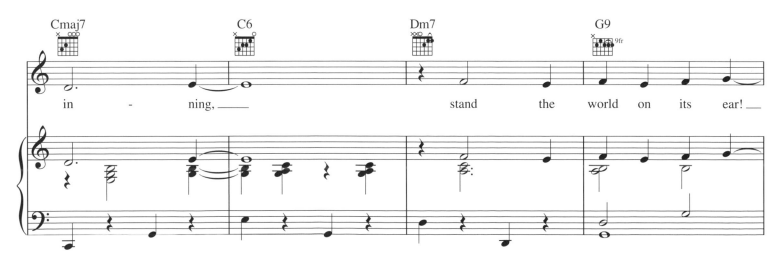

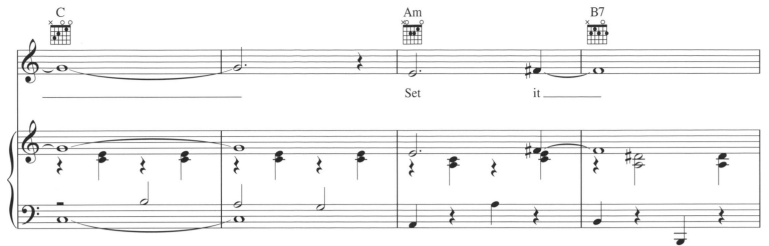

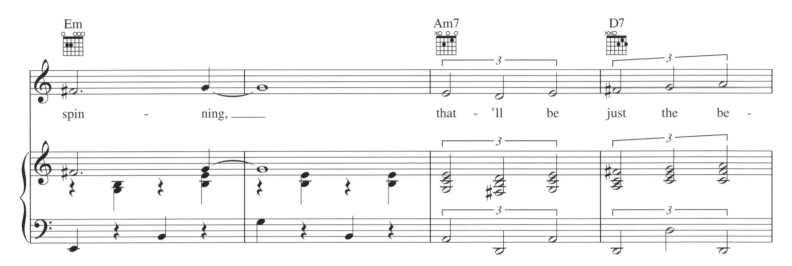

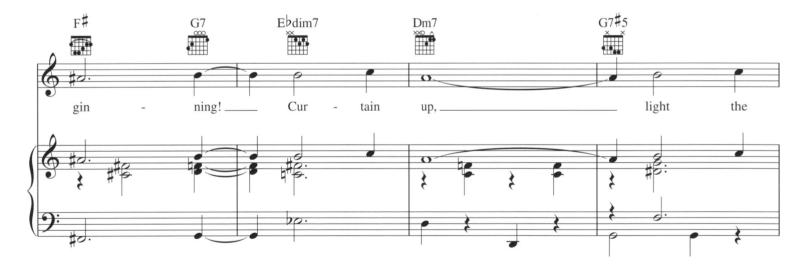

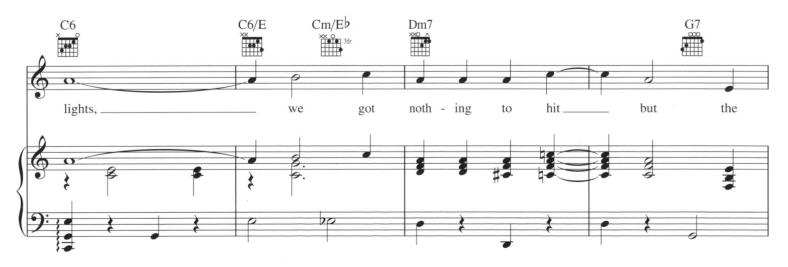

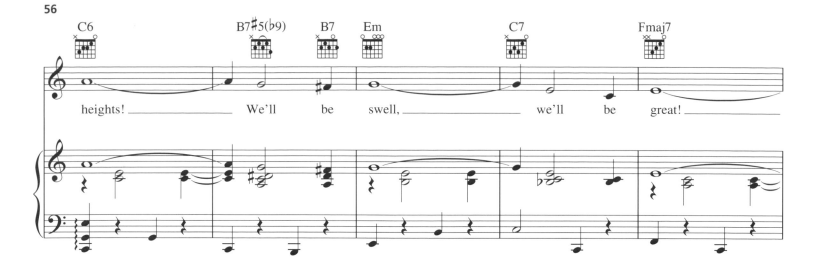

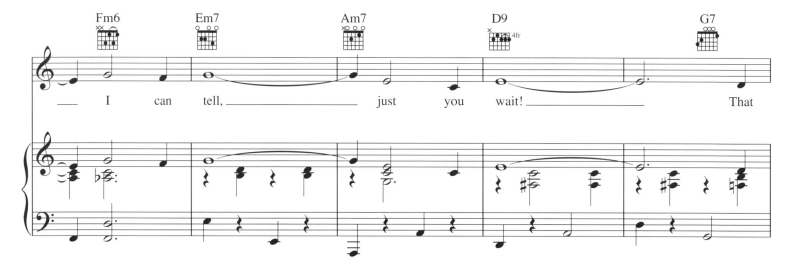

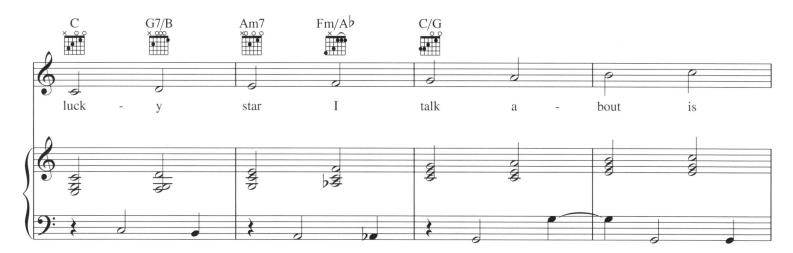

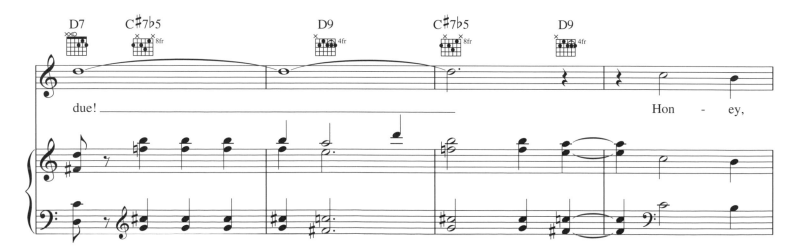

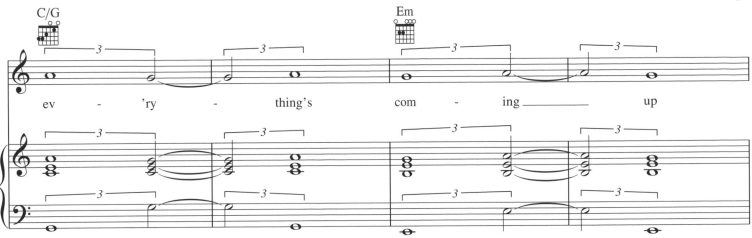

ev - 'ry - thing's com - ing _____ up

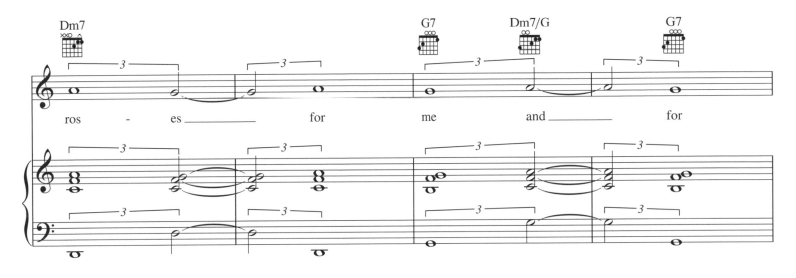

ros - es _____ for me and _____ for

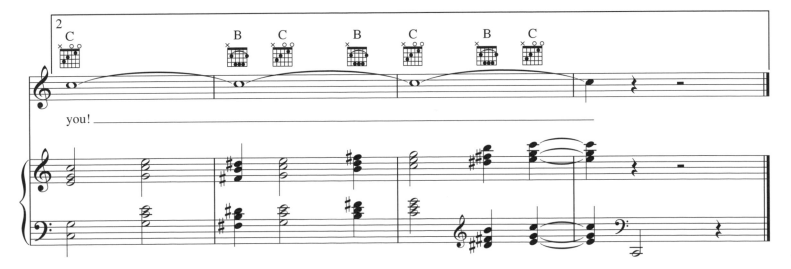

you! _____ Things look

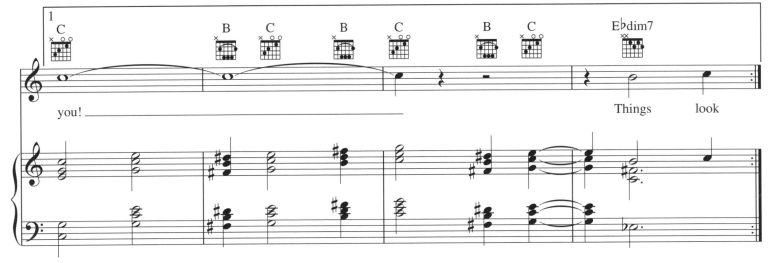

you! _____

FALLING IN LOVE WITH LOVE

from THE BOYS FROM SYRACUSE

Words by LORENZ HART
Music by RICHARD RODGERS

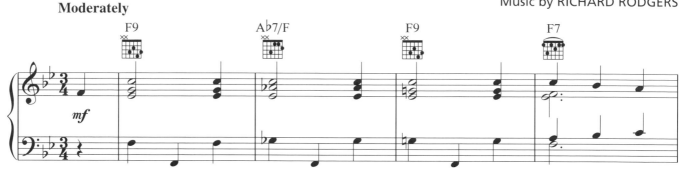

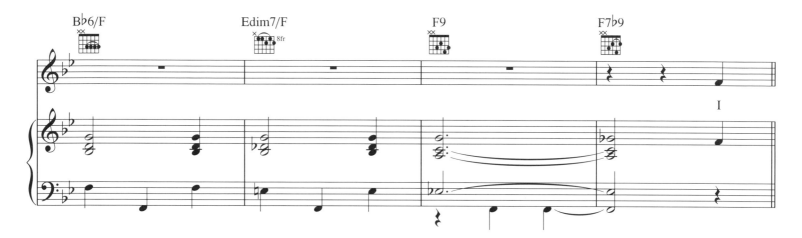

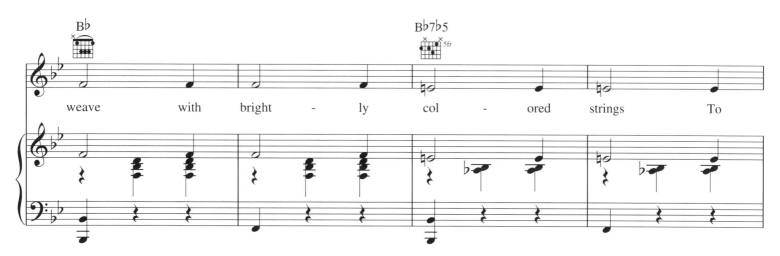

I weave with bright - ly col - ored strings To

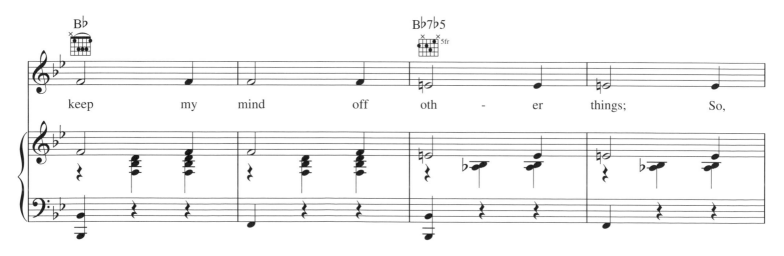

keep my mind off oth - er things; So,

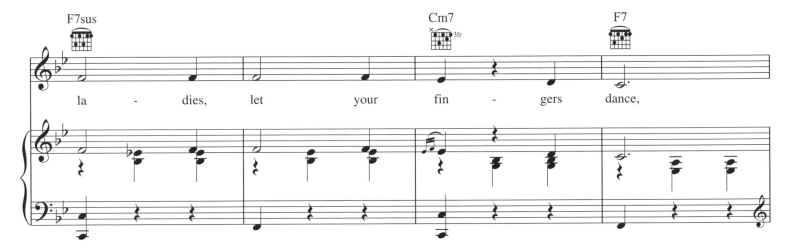

la - dies, let your fin - gers dance,

And

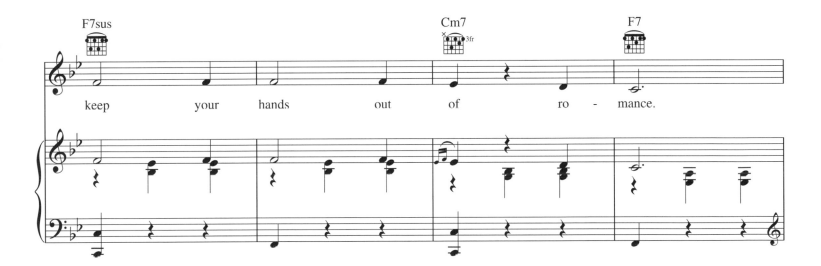

keep your hands out of ro - mance.

Love - ly

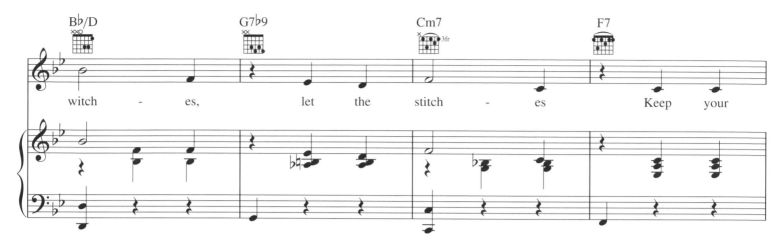

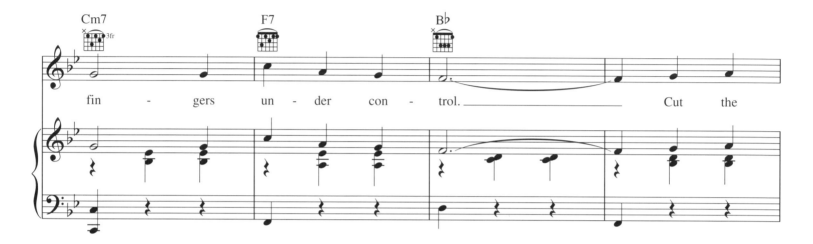

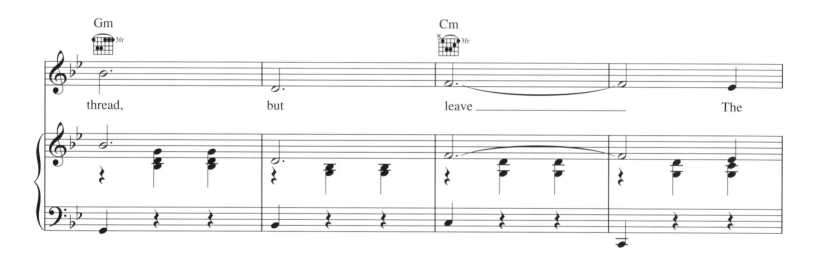

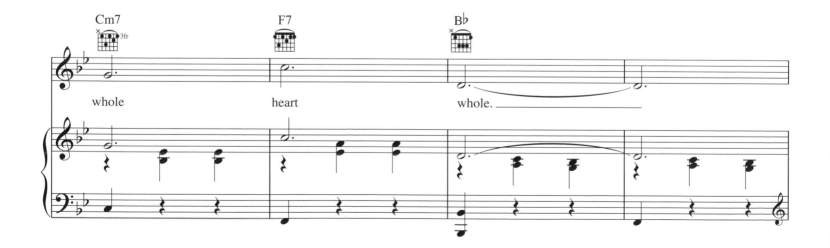

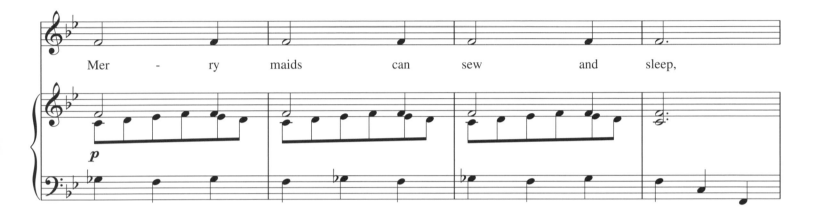

Mer - ry maids can sew and sleep,

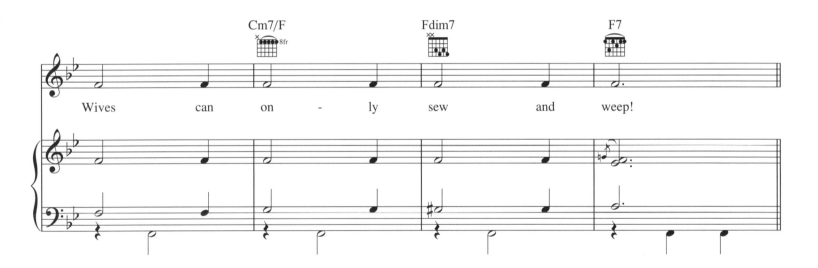

Wives can on - ly sew and weep!

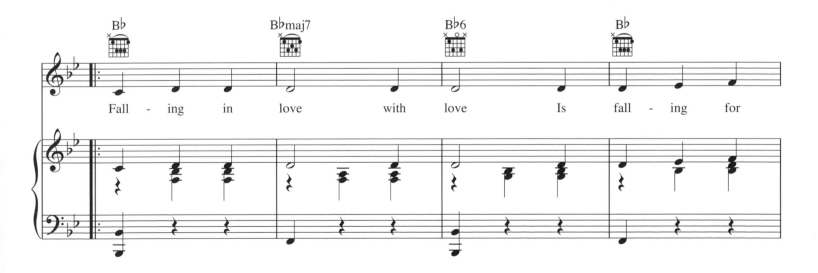

Fall - ing in love with love Is fall - ing for

62

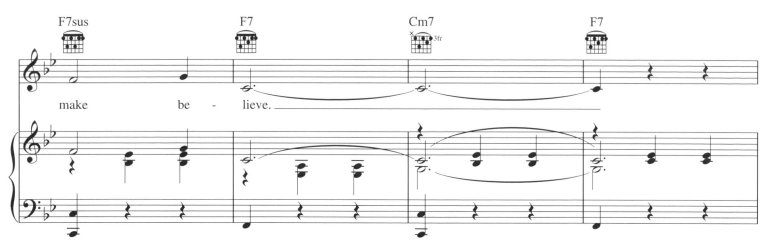

make be - lieve. _____

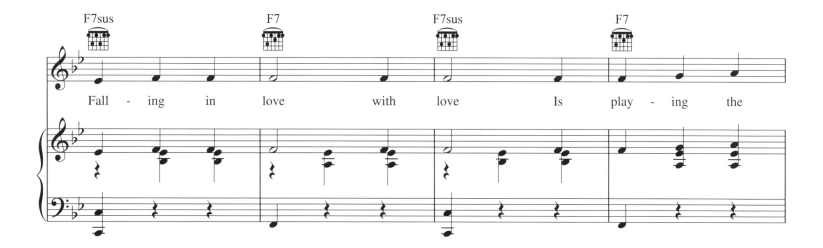

Fall - ing in love with love Is play - ing the

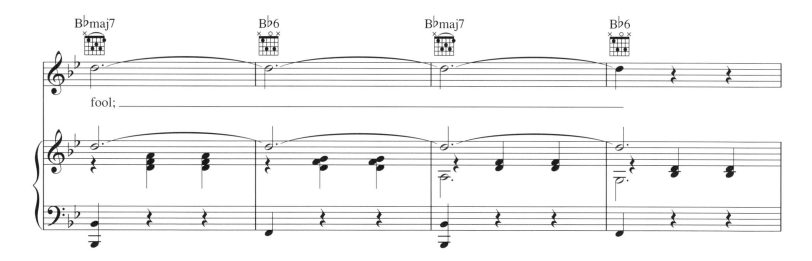

fool; _____

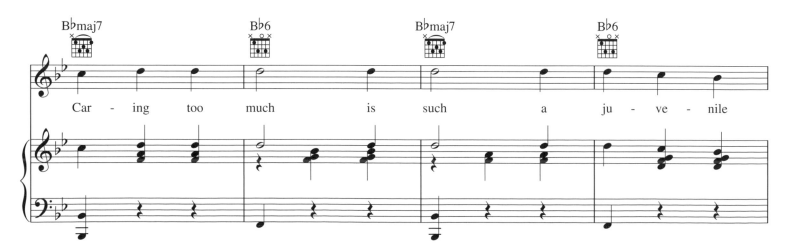

Car - ing too much is such a ju - ve - nile

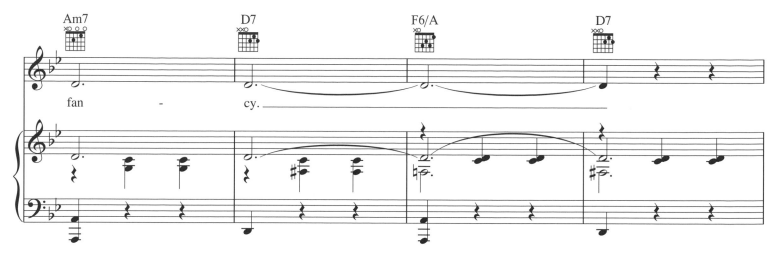

fan - cy. _____

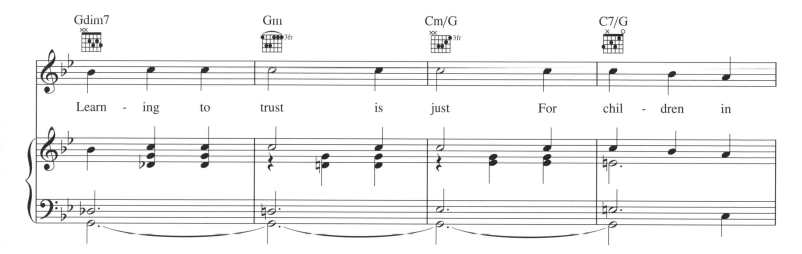

Learn - ing to trust is just For chil - dren in

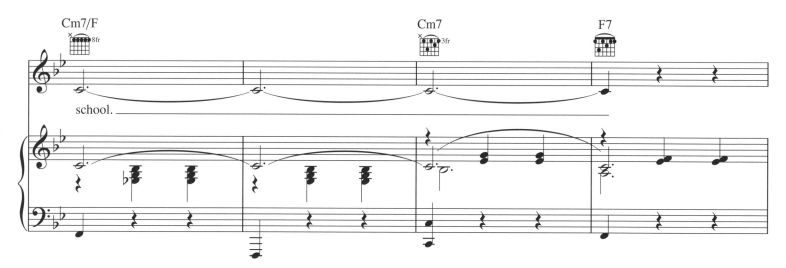

school. _____

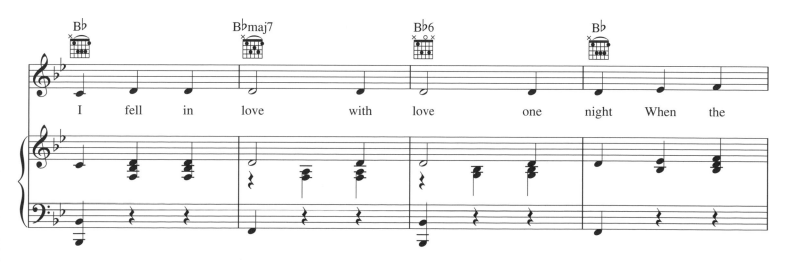

I fell in love with love one night When the

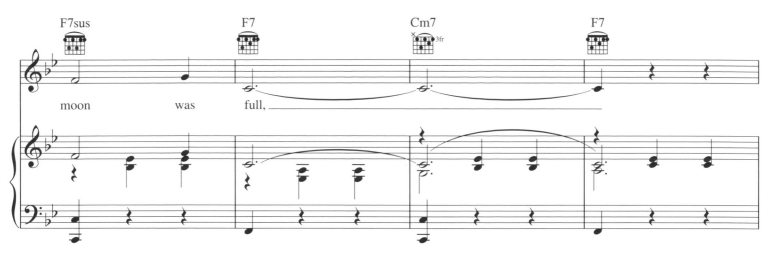

moon was full, _____

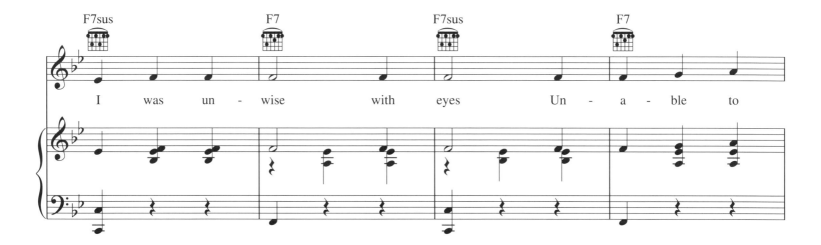

I was un - wise with eyes Un - a - ble to

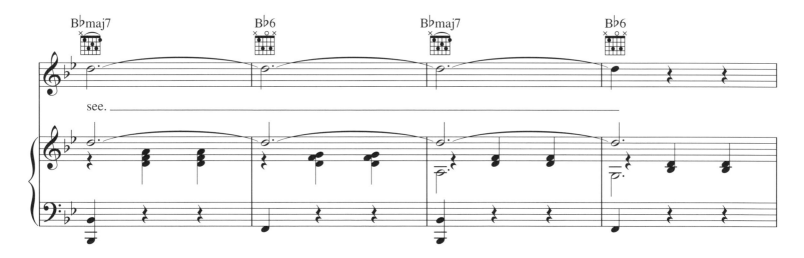

see. _____

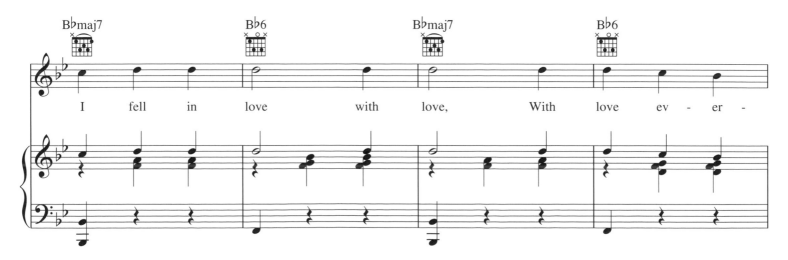

I fell in love with love, With love ev - er -

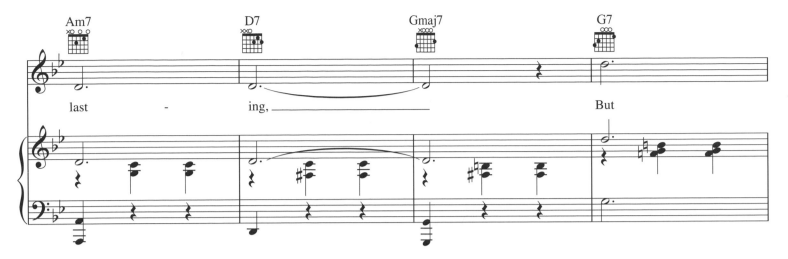

last - ing, _____ But

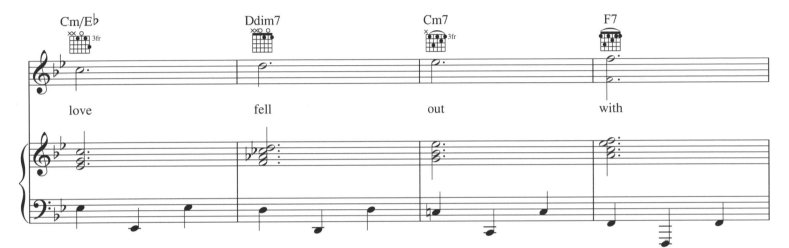

love fell out with

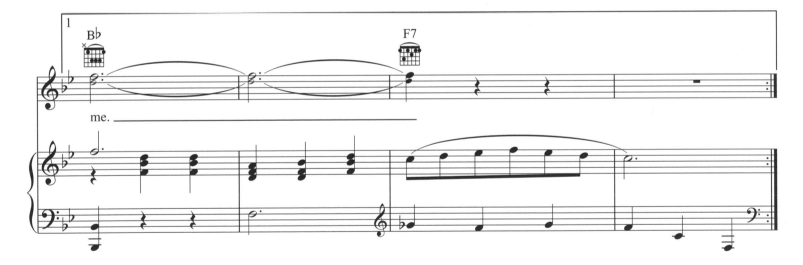

me. _____

me. _____

HELLO, DOLLY!

from HELLO, DOLLY!

Music and Lyric by
JERRY HERMAN

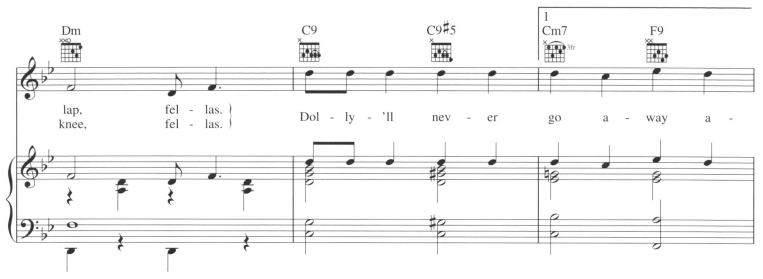

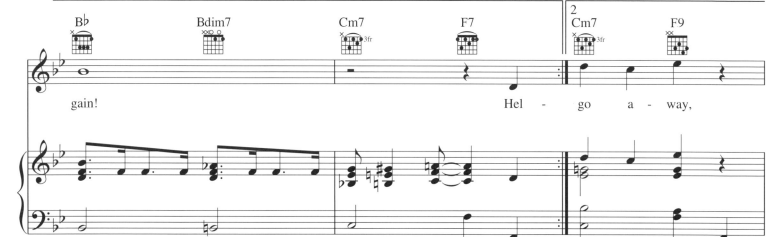

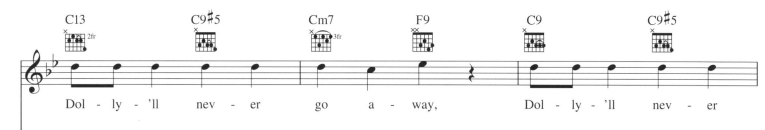

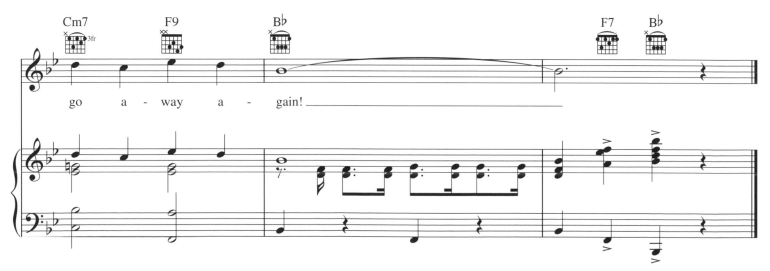

HONEYSUCKLE ROSE
from AIN'T MISBEHAVIN'

Words by ANDY RAZAF
Music by THOMAS "FATS" WALLER

Moderately, with a lilt

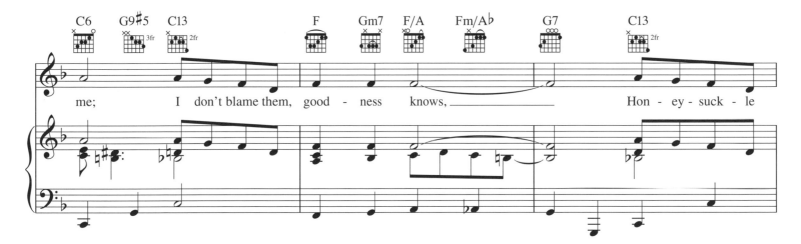

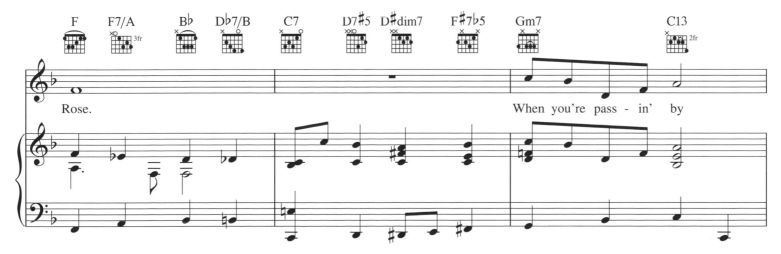

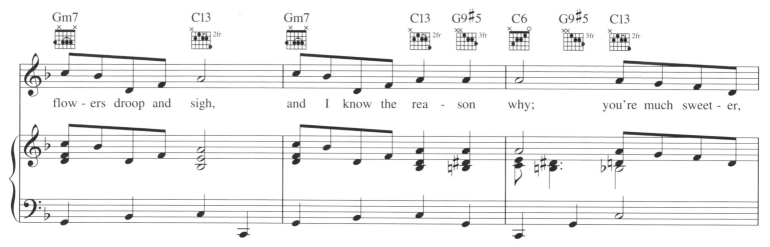

flow - ers droop and sigh, and I know the rea - son why; you're much sweet - er,

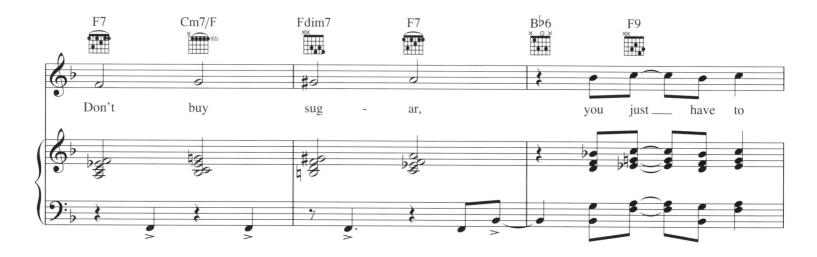

good - ness knows, _____ Hon - ey - suck - le Rose. _____

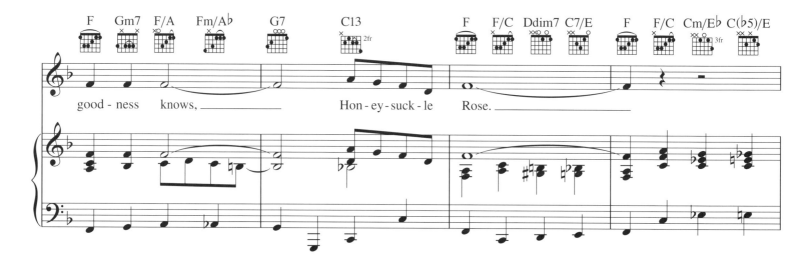

Don't buy sug - ar, you just ___ have to

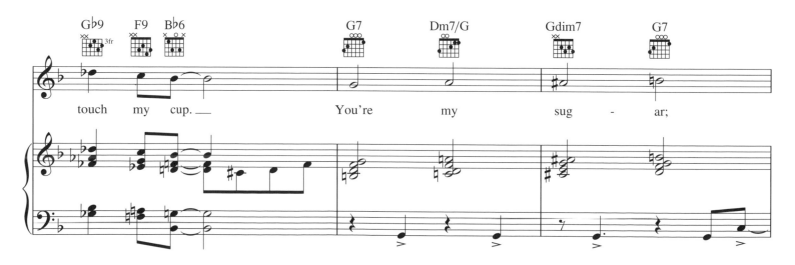

touch my cup. ___ You're my sug - ar;

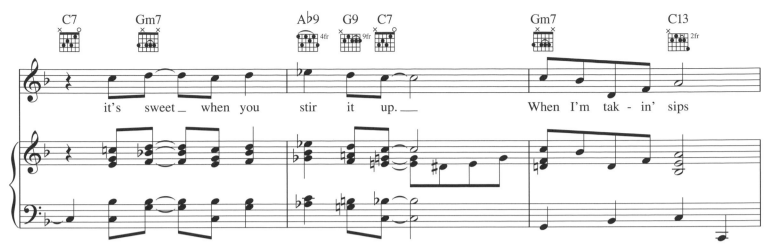

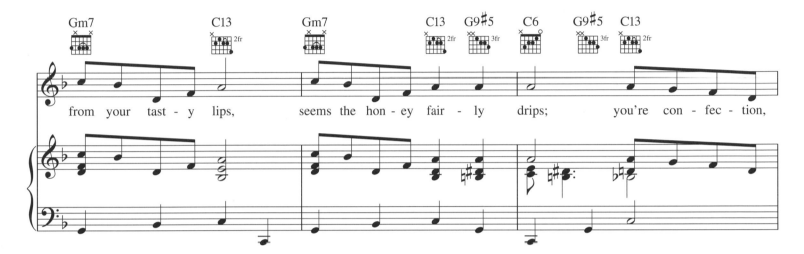

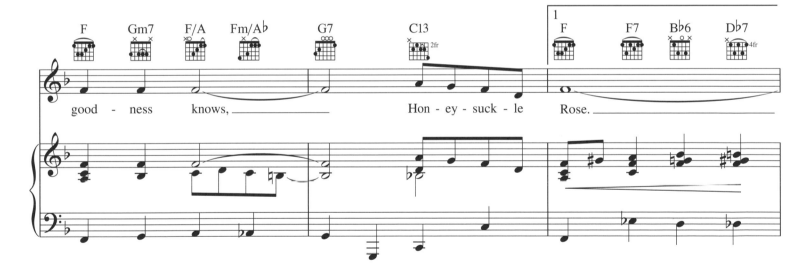

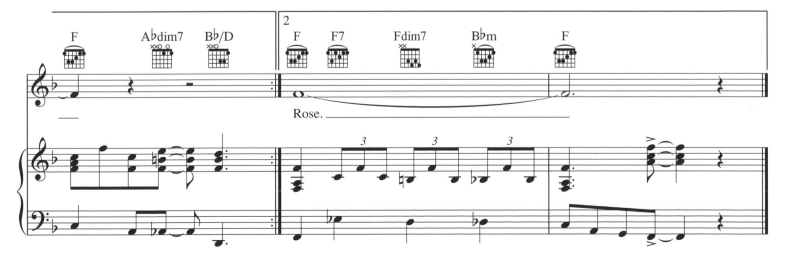

HELLO, YOUNG LOVERS

from THE KING AND I

Lyrics by OSCAR HAMMERSTEIN II
Music by RICHARD RODGERS

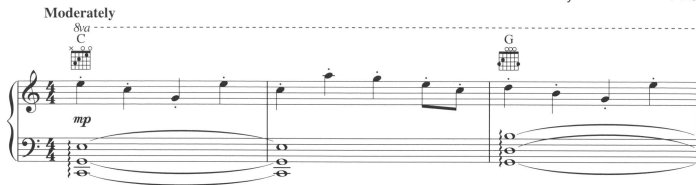

When I think of Tom I think a-bout a night When the

earth smelled of sum-mer, and the sky was streaked with white, and the soft mist of Eng-land was

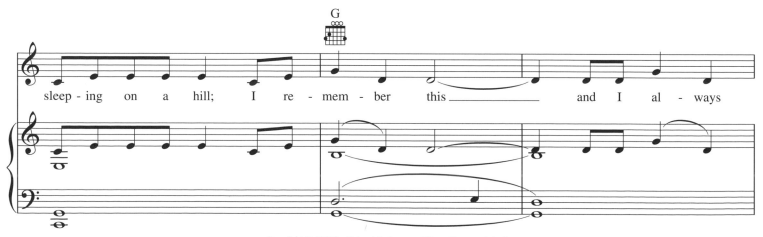

sleep-ing on a hill; I re-mem-ber this _____ and I al-ways

will. _____ There are new lov - ers now on the

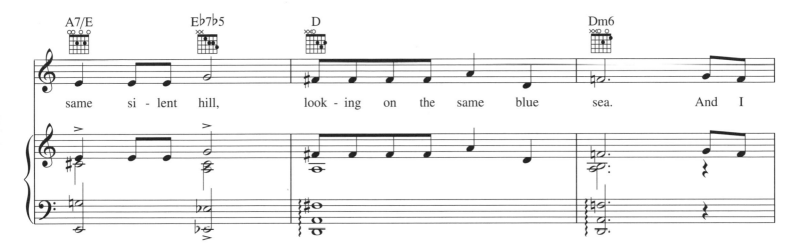

same si - lent hill, look - ing on the same blue sea. And I

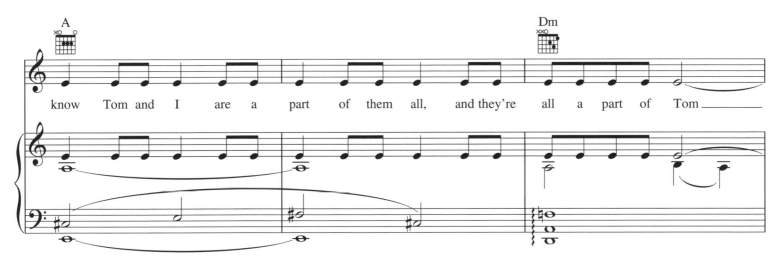

know Tom and I are a part of them all, and they're all a part of Tom _____

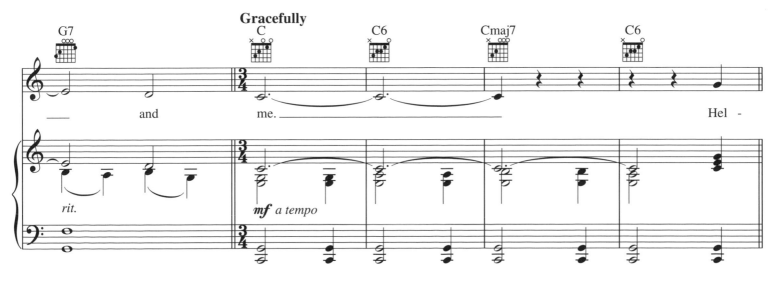

_____ and me. _____ Hel -

lo, young lov - ers, who - ev - er you are, I

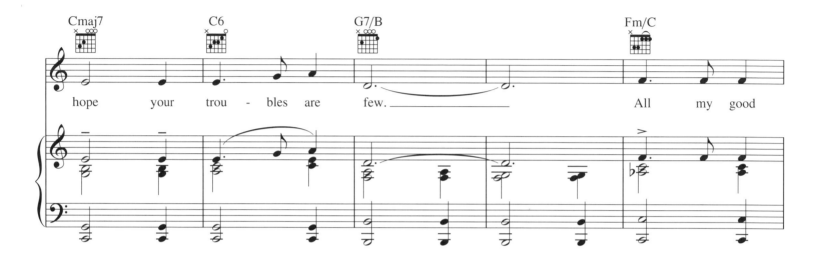

hope your trou - bles are few. _____ All my good

wish - es go with you to - night— I've been in love like

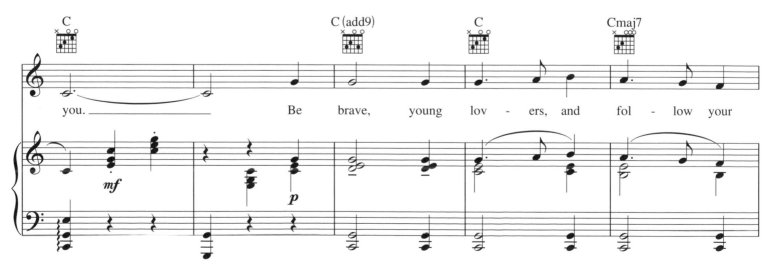

you. _____ Be brave, young lov - ers, and fol - low your

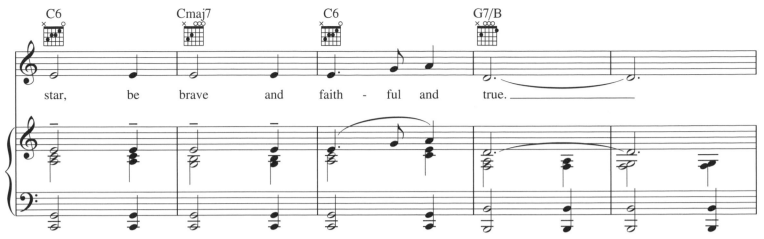

star, be brave and faith - ful and true.____

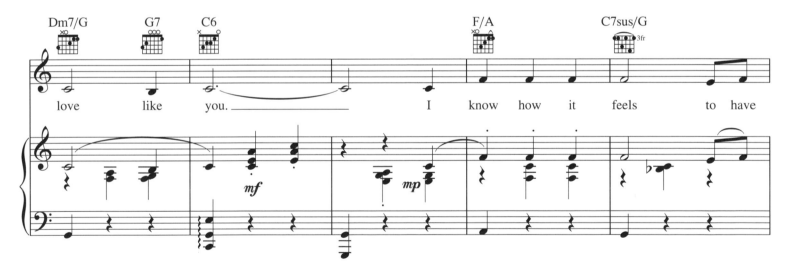

Cling ver - y close to each oth - er to - night— I've been in

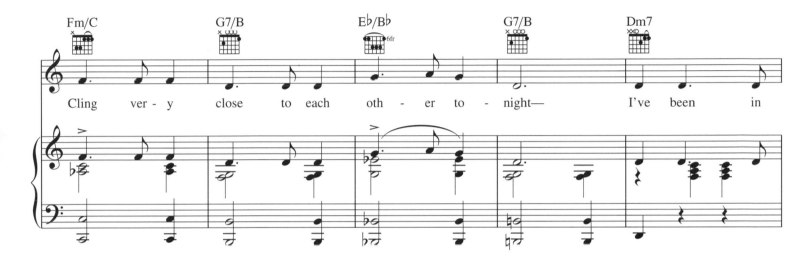

love like you.____ I know how it feels to have

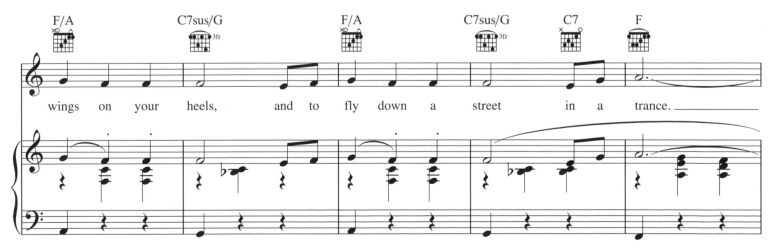

wings on your heels, and to fly down a street in a trance.____

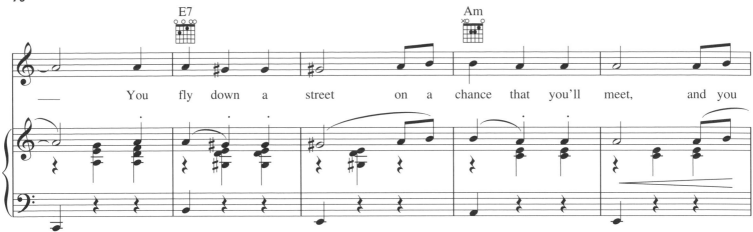

You fly down a street on a chance that you'll meet, and you

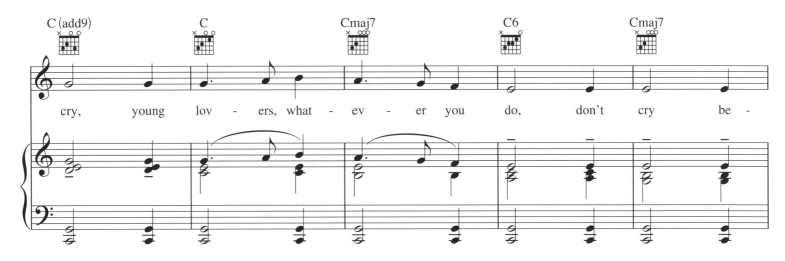

meet — not real - ly by chance. _____ Don't

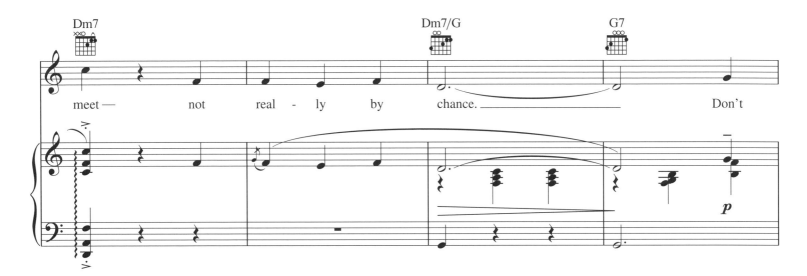

cry, young lov - ers, what - ev - er you do, don't cry be -

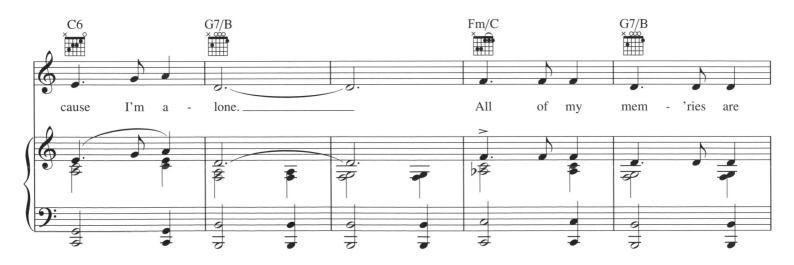

cause I'm a - lone. _____ All of my mem - 'ries are

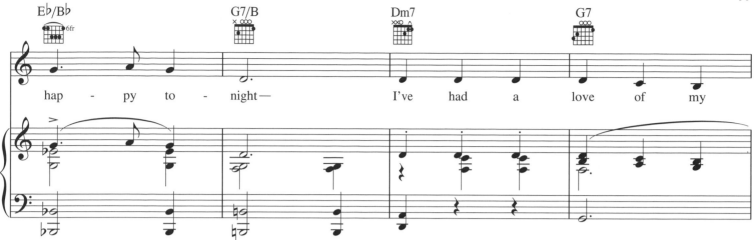

hap - py to - night— I've had a love of my

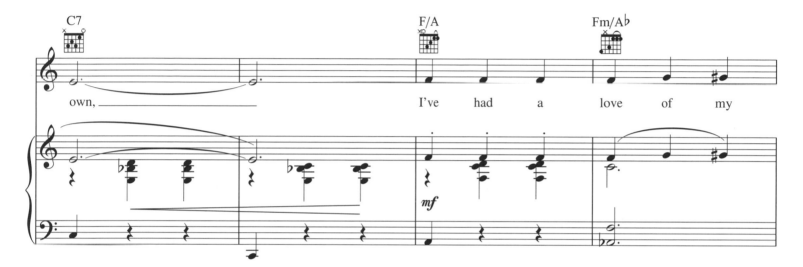

own, _____ I've had a love of my

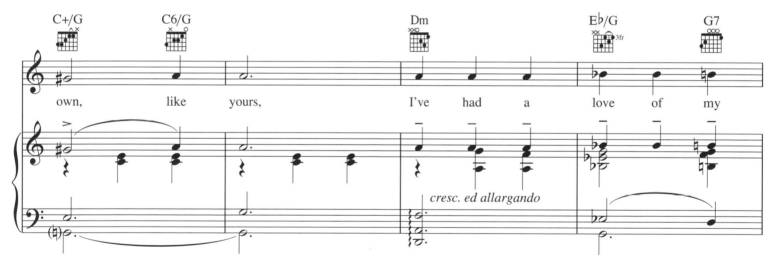

own, like yours, I've had a love of my

cresc. ed allargando

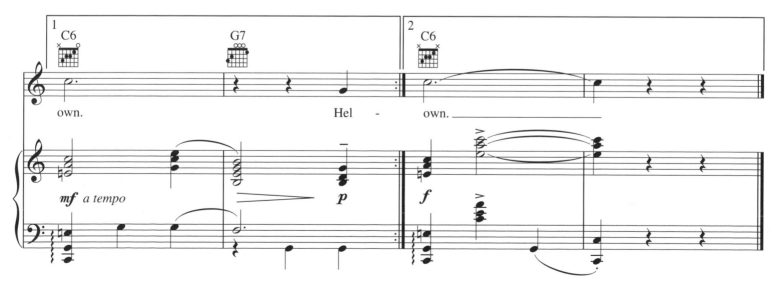

own. Hel - own. _____

mf a tempo

I BELIEVE IN YOU
from HOW TO SUCCEED IN BUSINESS WITHOUT REALLY TRYING

By FRANK LOESSER

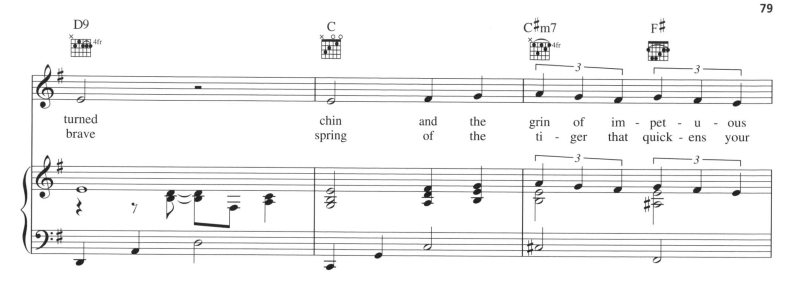

turned
brave

chin
spring

and
of

the
the

grin
ti -

of
ger

im -
that

pet - u - ous
quick - ens your

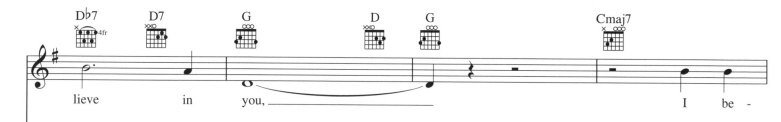

youth. }
walk. }

Oh, I be -

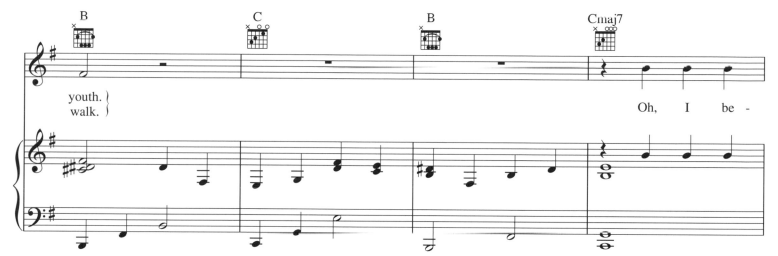

lieve

in

you, _____

I be -

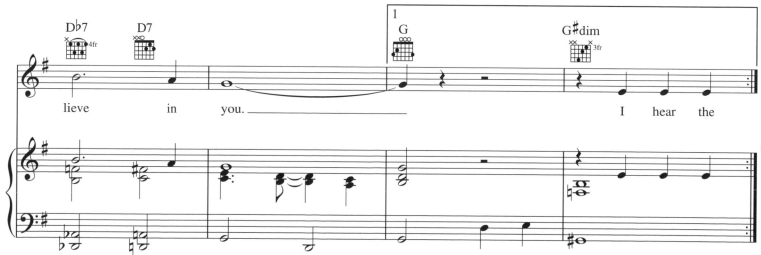

lieve

in

you. _____

I hear the

And when my faith in my

fel-low man _____ all but falls _____

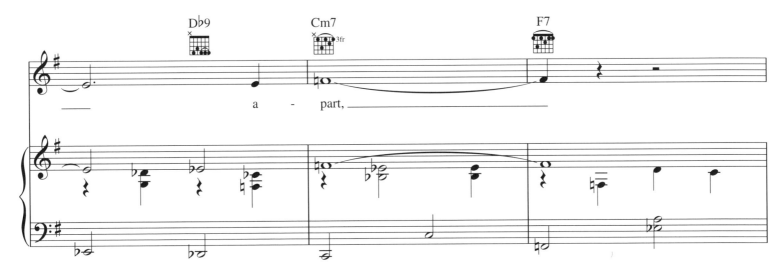

a - part, _____

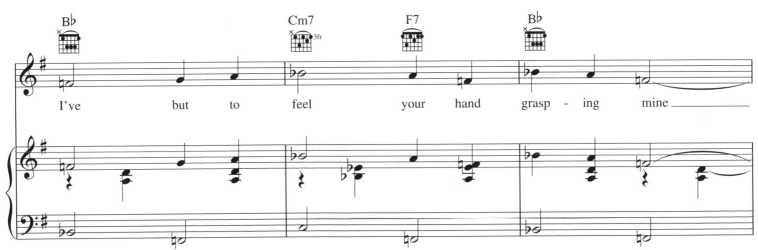

I've but to feel your hand grasp - ing mine _____

81

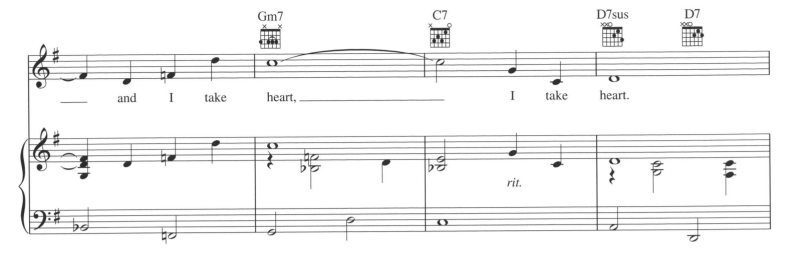

and I take heart, _____ I take heart.

To see the cool clear eyes of a

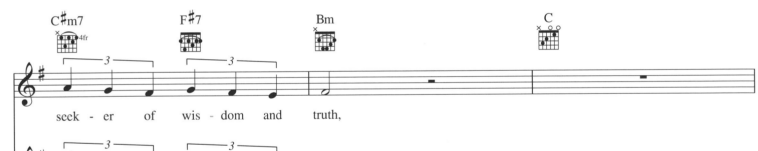

seck - er of wis - dom and truth,

yet there's that slam bang

tang rem - i - nis - cent of gin and ver - mouth.

Oh, I be - lieve in

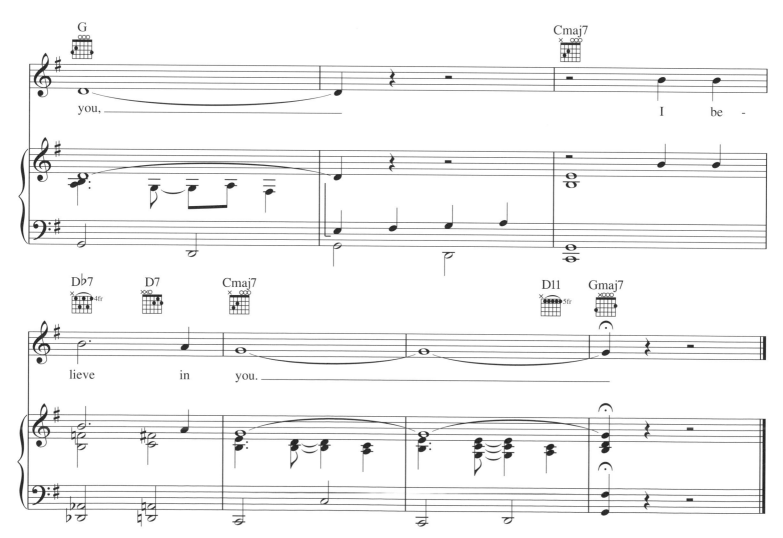

you, _____ I be -

lieve in you. _____

IF EVER I WOULD LEAVE YOU

from CAMELOT

Words by ALAN JAY LERNER
Music by FREDERICK LOEWE

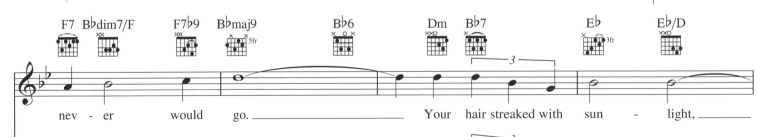

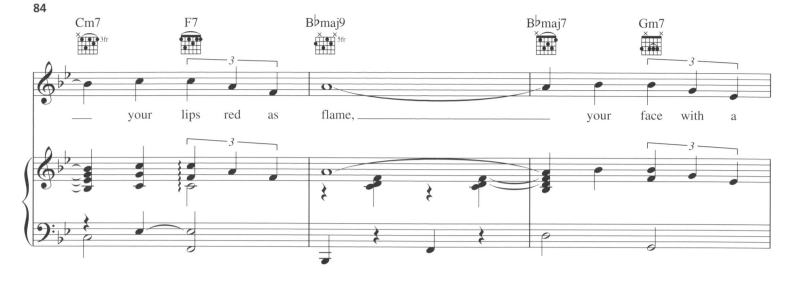

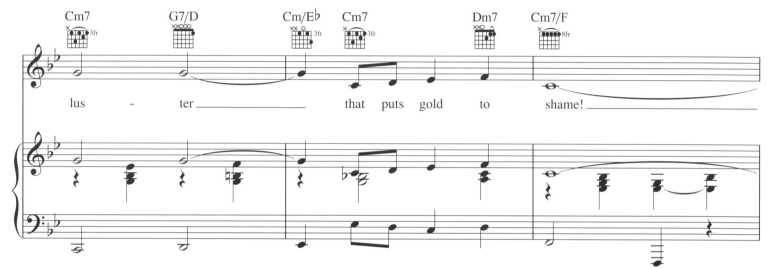

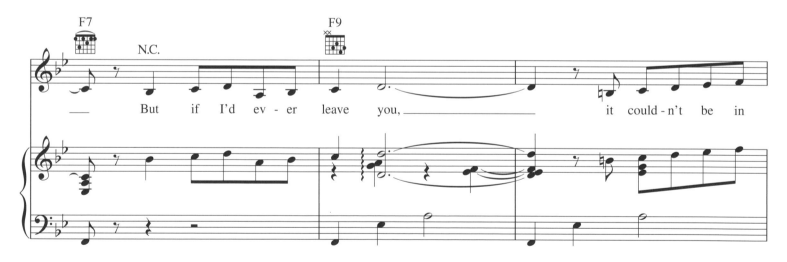

win - try eve - ning when you catch the fi - re's glow? _____

___ If ev - er I would leave you, _____ how could it be in

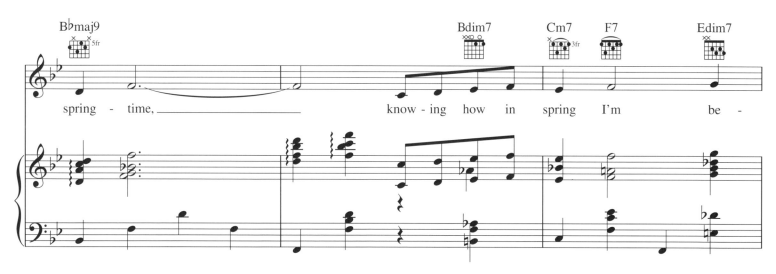

spring - time, _____ know - ing how in spring I'm be -

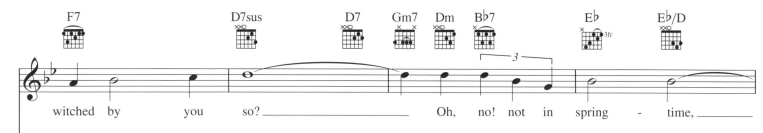

witched by you so? _____ Oh, no! not in spring - time, _____

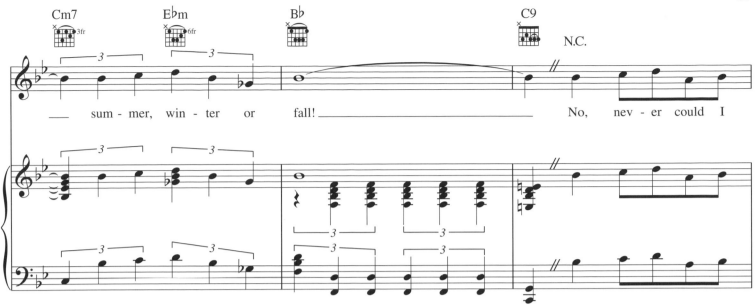

sum - mer, win - ter or fall! _____ No, nev - er could I

leave you _____ at all! _____ And could I

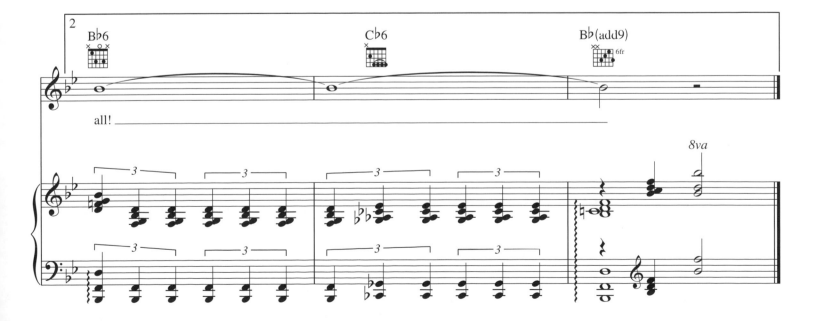

all! _____

I DON'T KNOW HOW TO LOVE HIM

from JESUS CHRIST SUPERSTAR

Words by TIM RICE
Music by ANDREW LLOYD WEBBER

seen my-self, I seem like some-one else.

I don't know how to take this I don't see why he

moves me. He's a man, he's just a man, and I've

had so man-y _____ men be-fore in ver-y man-y

I DREAMED A DREAM
from LES MISÉRABLES

Music by CLAUDE-MICHEL SCHÖNBERG
Lyrics by ALAIN BOUBLIL,
JEAN-MARC NATEL and HERBERT KRETZMER

Fantine: I dreamed a dream in days gone by, when hope was high and life worth living. I dreamed that love would never

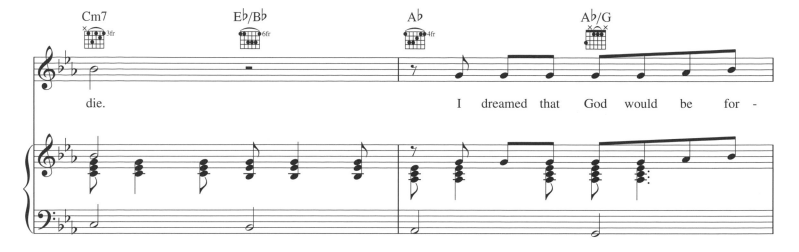

die.　I dreamed that God would be for -

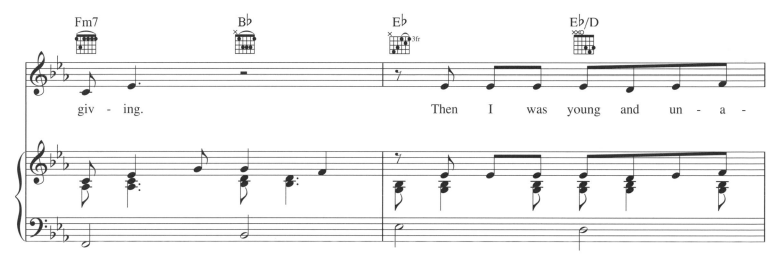

giv - ing.　Then I was young and un - a -

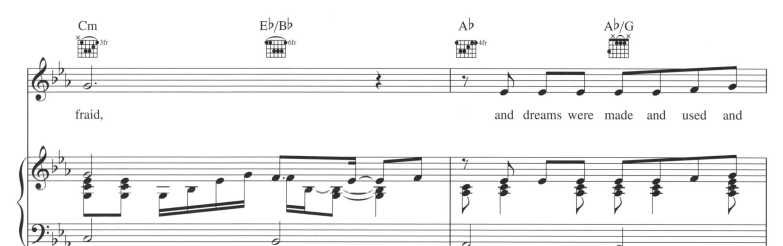

fraid,　and dreams were made and used and

wast - ed. _____　There was no ran - som to be

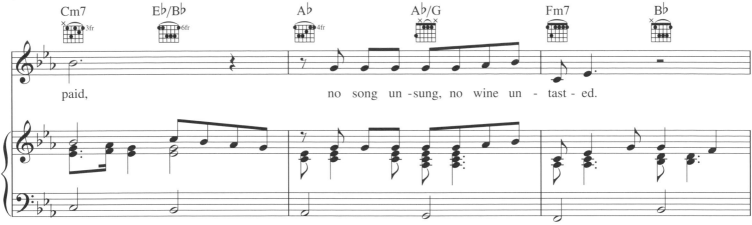

paid,   no song un-sung, no wine un - tast - ed.

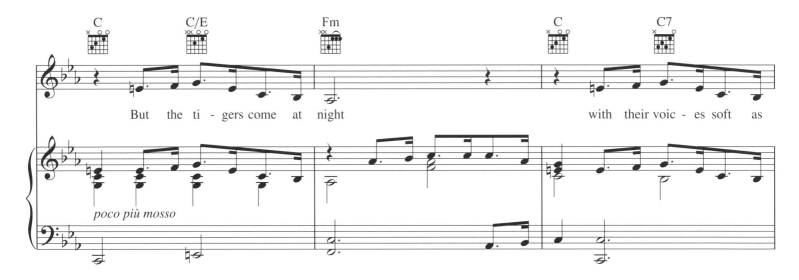

But the ti - gers come at night   with their voic - es soft as

poco più mosso

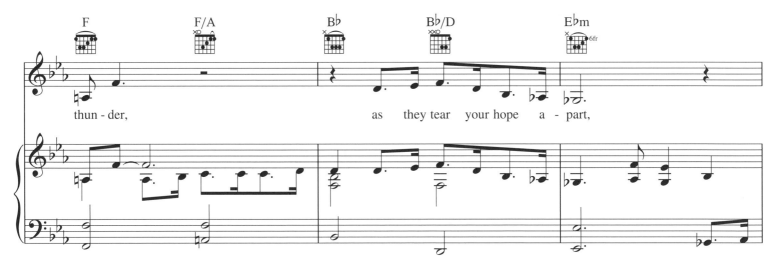

thun - der,   as they tear your hope a - part,

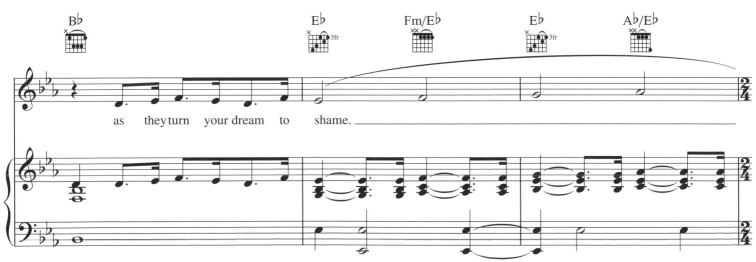

as they turn your dream to shame.

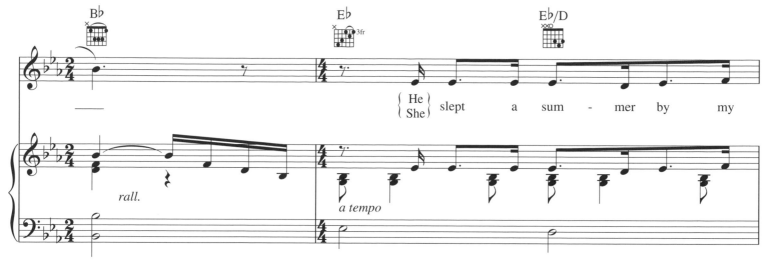

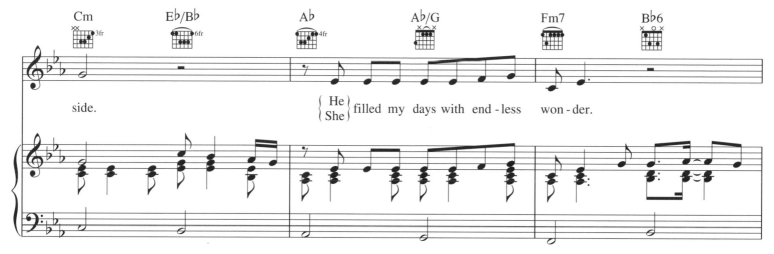

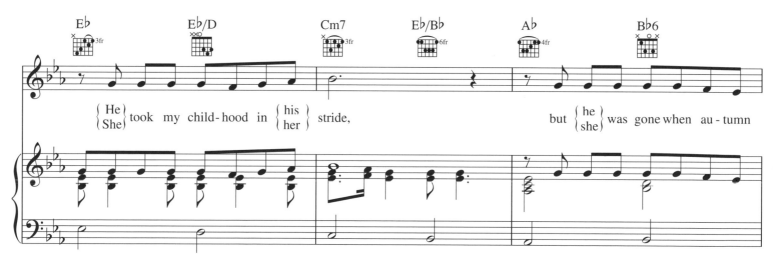

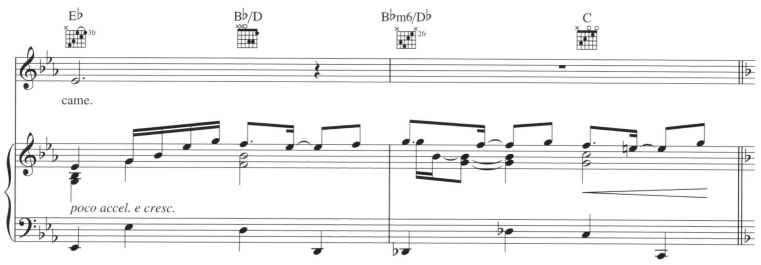

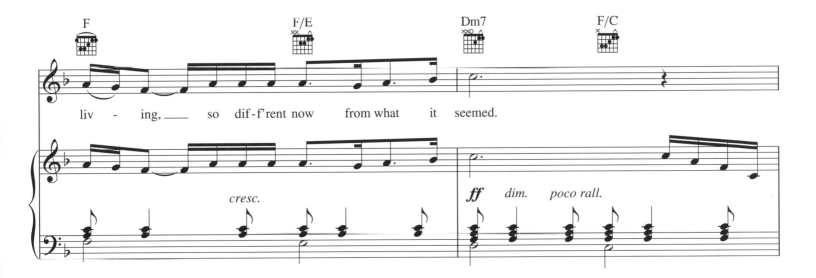

I ENJOY BEING A GIRL

from FLOWER DRUM SONG

Lyrics by OSCAR HAMMERSTEIN II
Music by RICHARD RODGERS

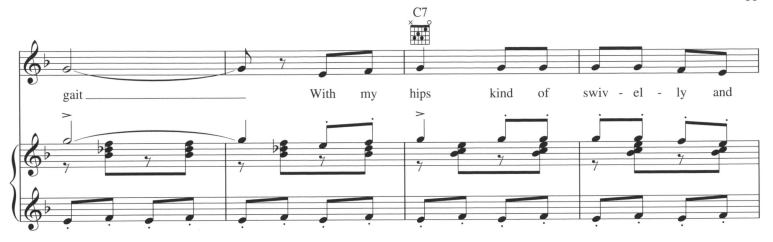

gait _____ With my hips kind of swiv-el-ly and

swerv - y._____ I a - dore be - ing dressed in some - thing

fril - ly _____ When my date comes to get me at my place. Out I

go with my Joe or John or Bill - y, _____ Like a fil - ly who is

ready for the race! _____ When

Refrain *(brightly)*

I have a brand-new hair-do _____ With my

eye-lash-es all in curl, _____ I

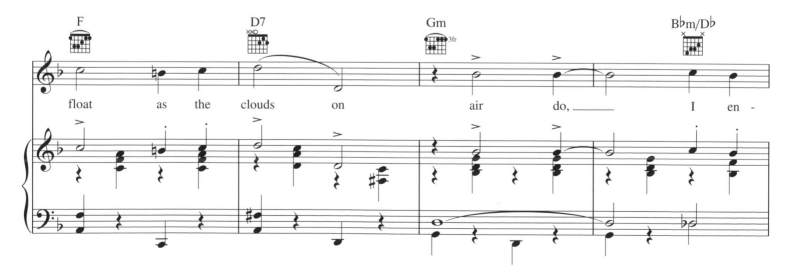

float as the clouds on air do, _____ I en-

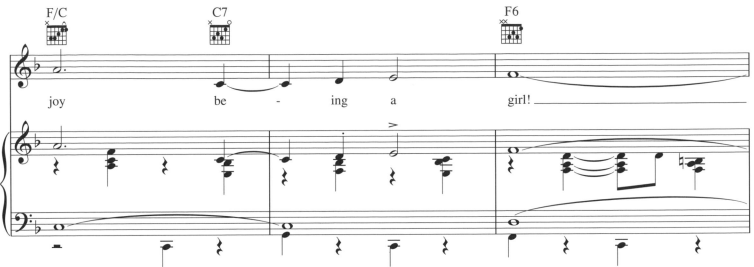

joy be - ing a girl!

When men say I'm cute and

fun - ny And my teeth are - n't

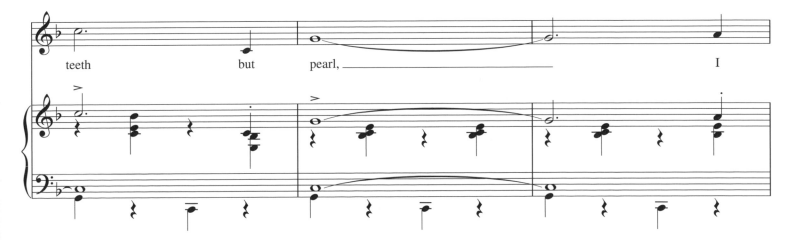

teeth but pearl, I

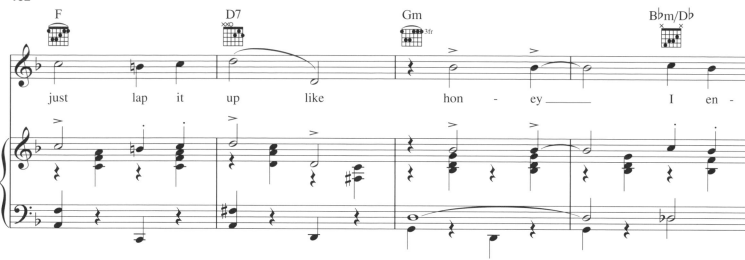

just lap it up like hon - ey _____ I en -

joy be - ing a girl! _____

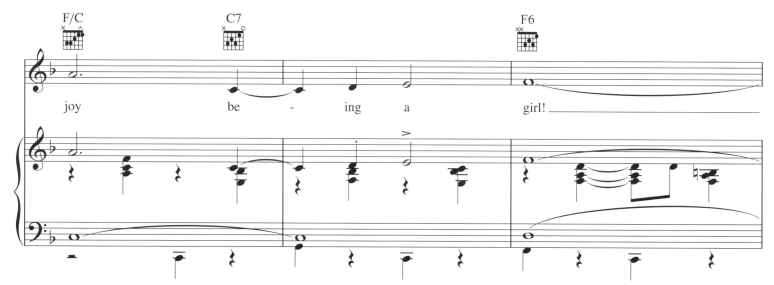

_____ I flip when a fel - low sends me

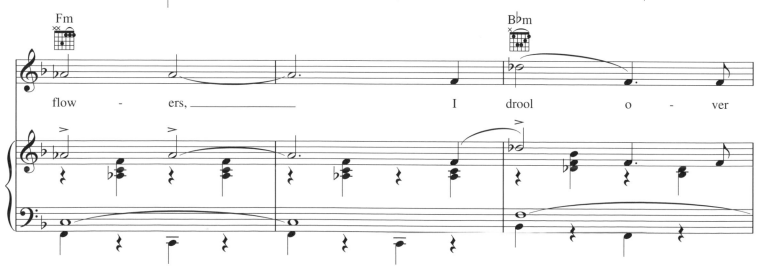

flow - ers, _____ I drool o - ver

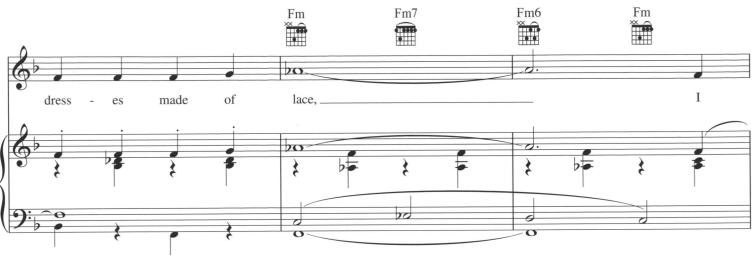

dress - es made of lace, _____ I

talk on the tel - e - phone for ho - urs _____

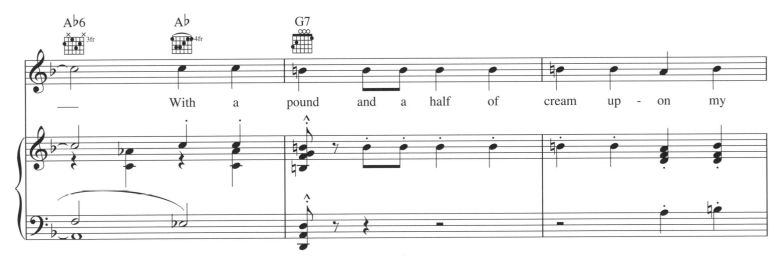

___ With a pound and a half of cream up - on my

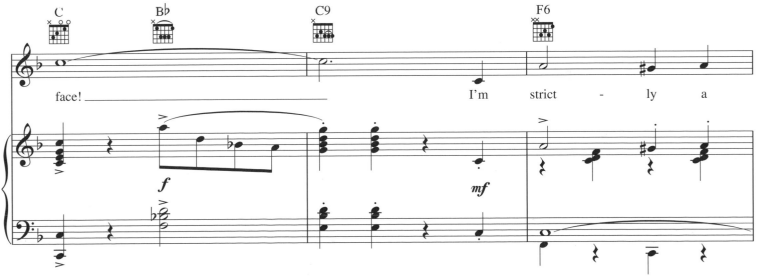

face! _____ I'm strict - ly a

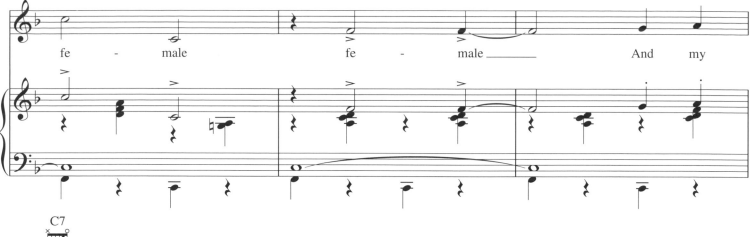

fe - male   fe - male _____   And my

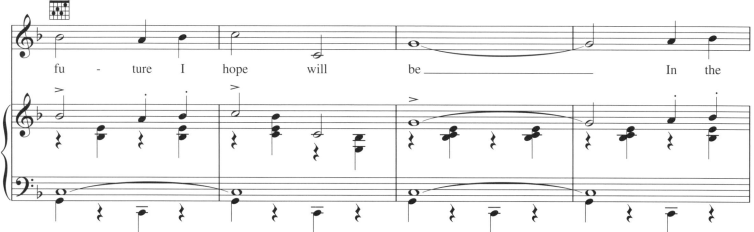

fu - ture I hope will be _____ In the

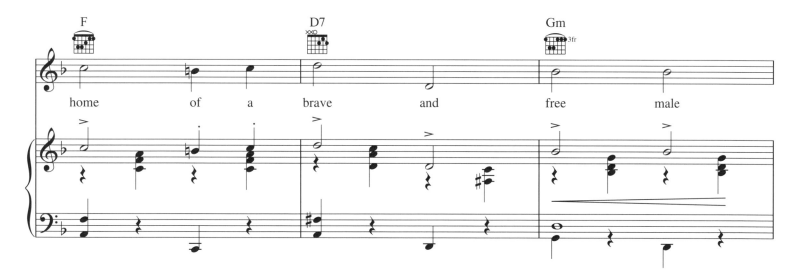

home of a brave and free male

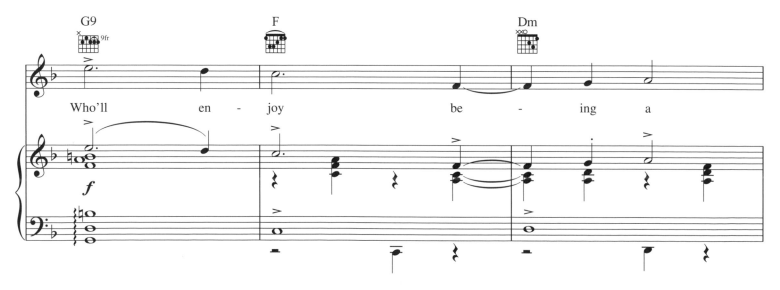

Who'll en - joy be - ing a

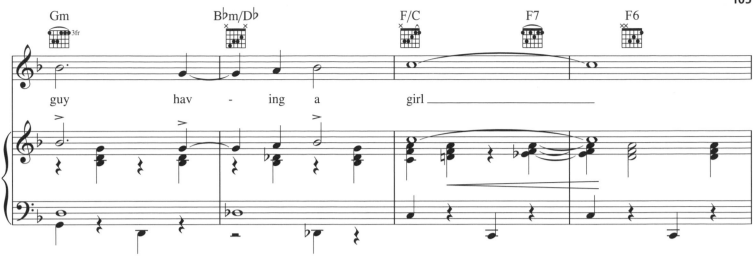

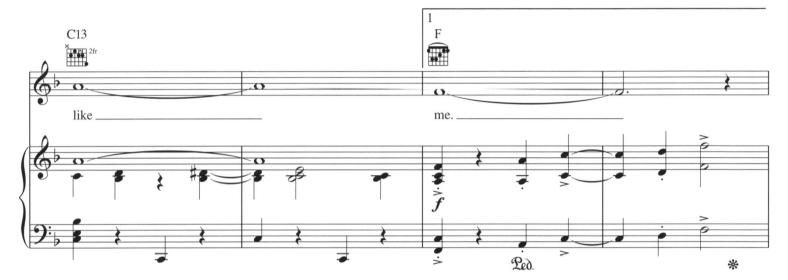

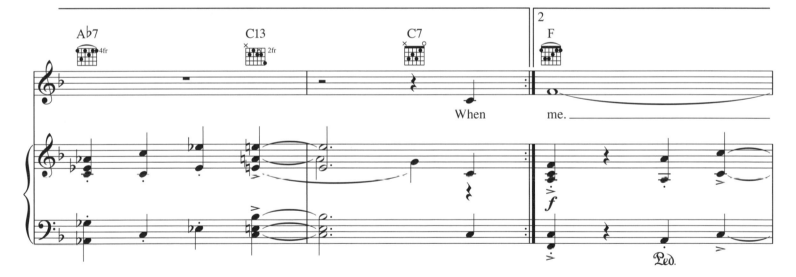

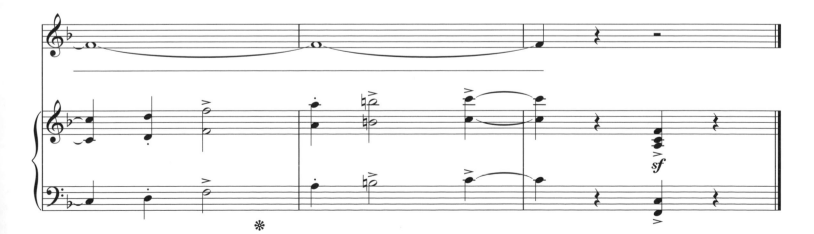

IF I WERE A BELL

from GUYS AND DOLLS

By FRANK LOESSER

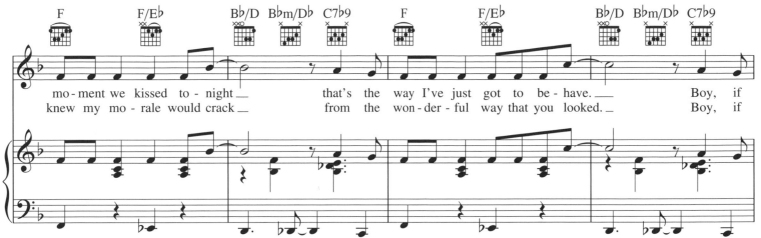

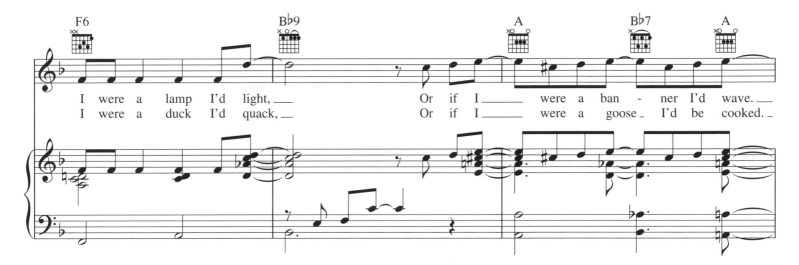

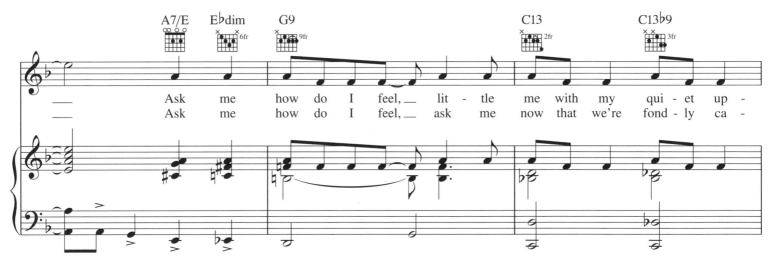

JUST IN TIME
from BELLS ARE RINGING

Words by BETTY COMDEN and ADOLPH GREEN
Music by JULE STYNE

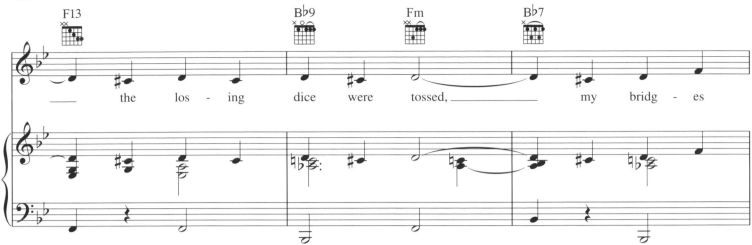

the los - ing dice were tossed, _____ my bridg - es

all were crossed, _____ no - where to go. _____

Now you're here, _____ and now I

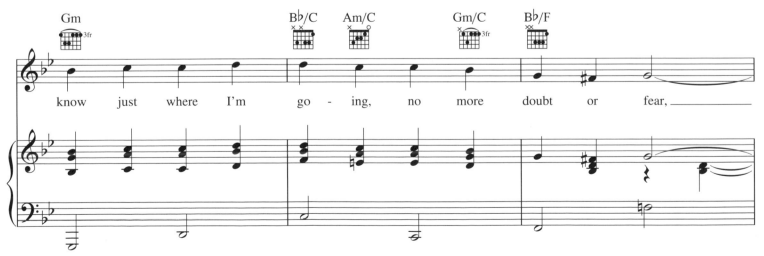

know just where I'm go - ing, no more doubt or fear, _____

111

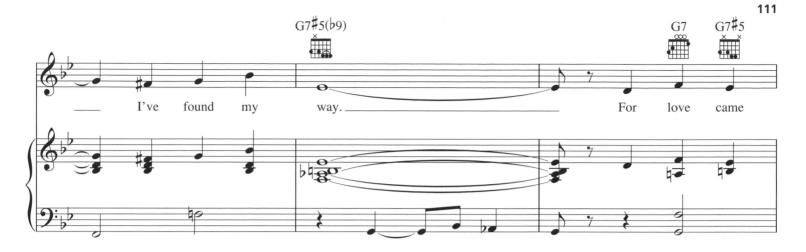

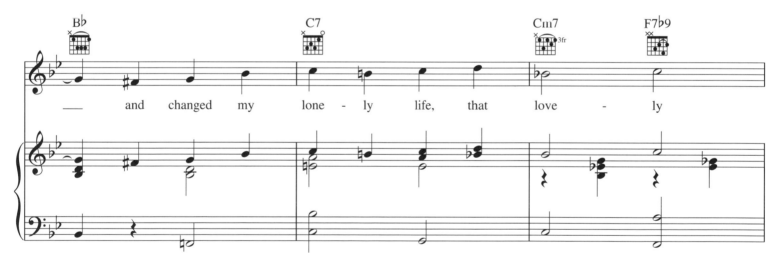

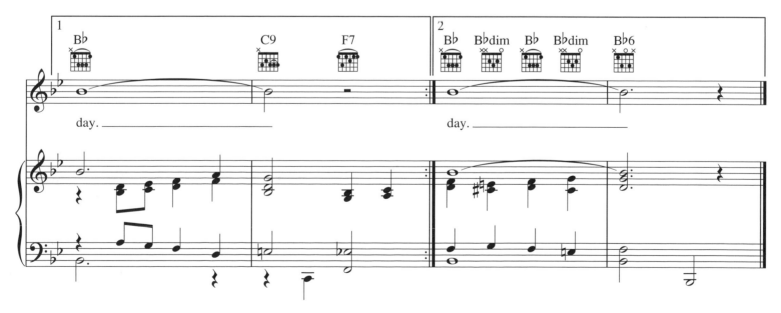

THE IMPOSSIBLE DREAM
(The Quest)
from MAN OF LA MANCHA

Lyric by JOE DARION
Music by MITCH LEIGH

Tempo di Bolero

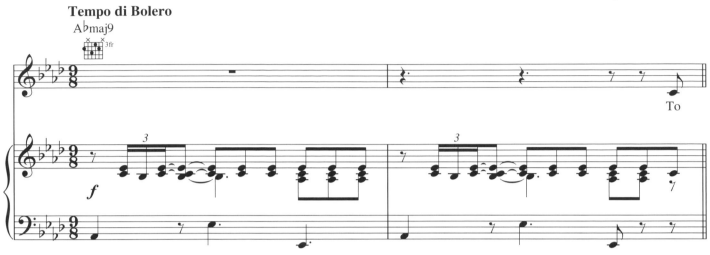

dream _____ the im-pos-si-ble dream, _____ to
right _____ the un-right-a-ble wrong, _____ to

fight _____ the un-beat-a-ble foe, _____ to
love _____ pure and chaste from a - far, _____ to

bear _____ with un-bear-a-ble sor-row, _____ to
try _____ when your arms are too wea-ry, _____ to

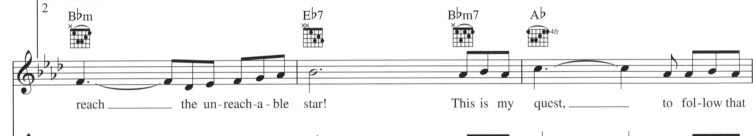

1
run _____ where the brave dare not go. _____ To

2
reach _____ the un-reach-a-ble star! This is my quest, _____ to fol-low that

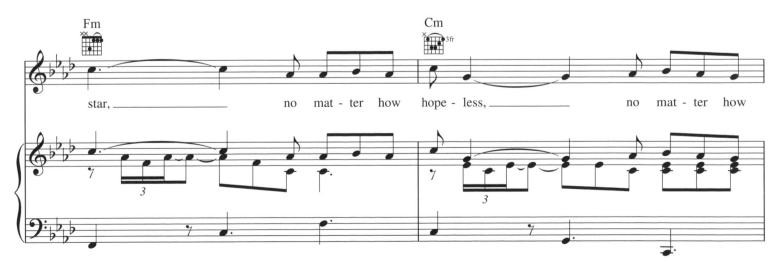

star, _____ no mat-ter how hope-less, _____ no mat-ter how

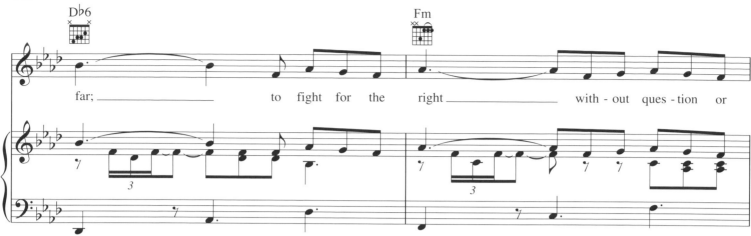

far; _____ to fight for the right _____ with-out ques-tion or

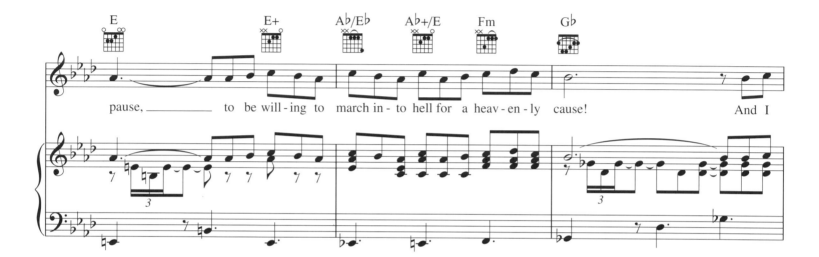

pause, _____ to be will-ing to march in-to hell for a heav-en-ly cause! And I

know, _____ if I'll on-ly be true _____ to this glo-ri-ous

quest, _____ that my heart _____ will lie peace-ful and

THE LAST NIGHT OF THE WORLD

from MISS SAIGON

Music by CLAUDE-MICHEL SCHÖNBERG
Lyrics by RICHARD MALTBY JR. and ALAIN BOUBLIL
Adapted from original French Lyrics by ALAIN BOUBLIL

Languidly

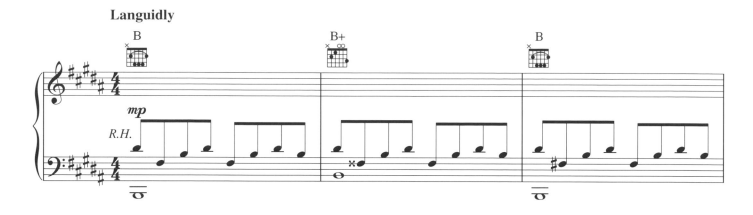

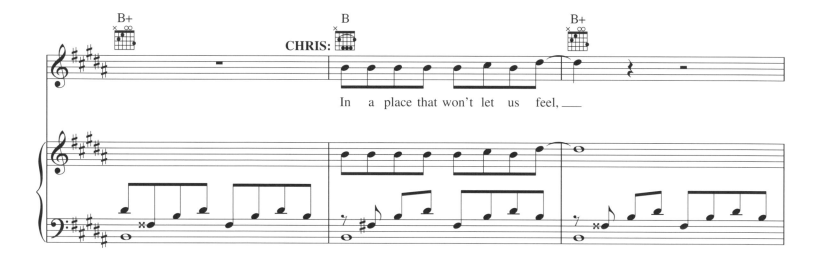

In a place that won't let us feel, ___

in a life where noth-ing seems real ___ I have found you, ___

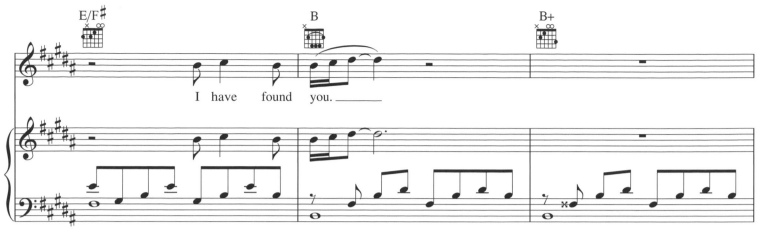

I have found you. _____

KIM:

In a world that's mov ing too fast, ___ in a world where noth ing can last, __

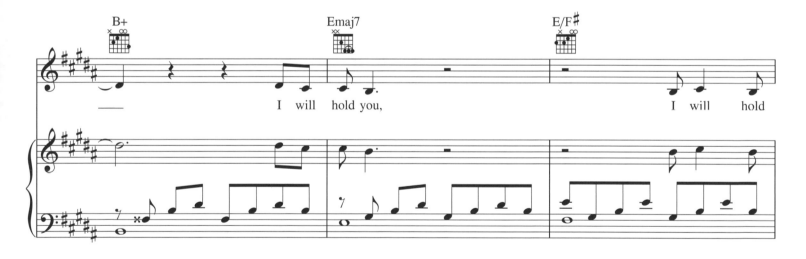

___ I will hold you, I will hold

CHRIS:

you. _____ Our lives will change when to - mor-row comes. __ KIM: To-night our

118

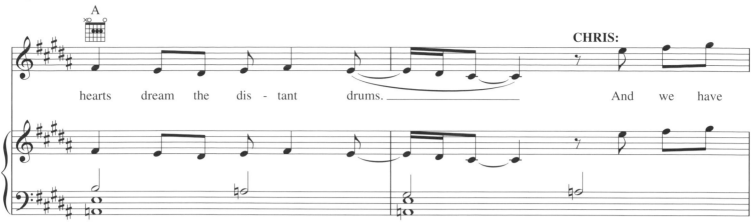

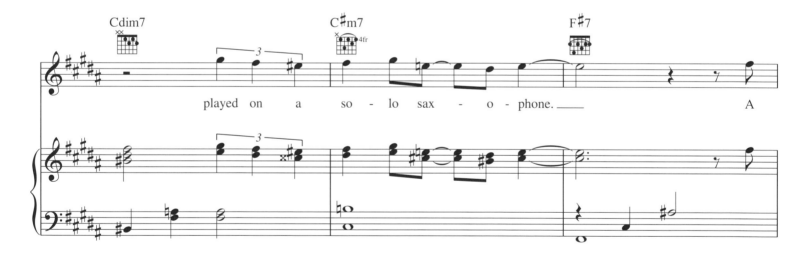

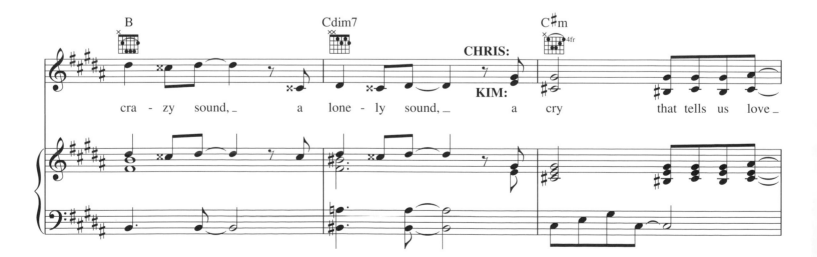

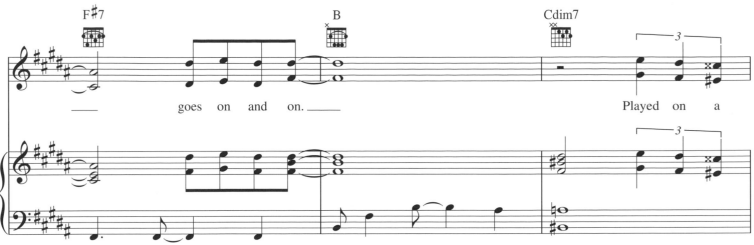

goes on and on. _____ Played on a

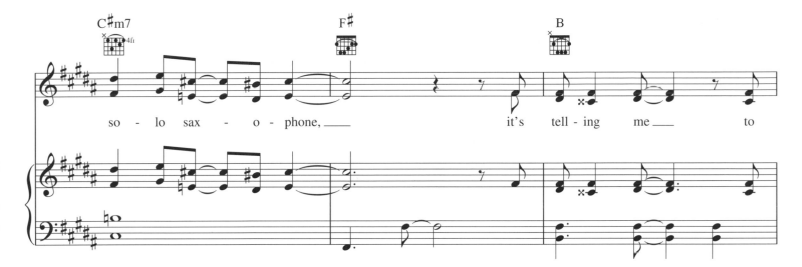

so - lo sax - o - phone, _____ it's tell - ing me ___ to

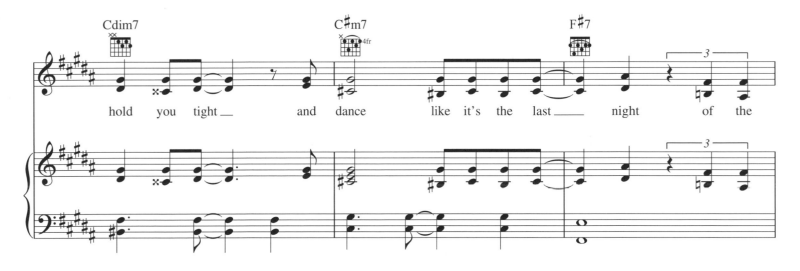

hold you tight ___ and dance like it's the last ___ night of the

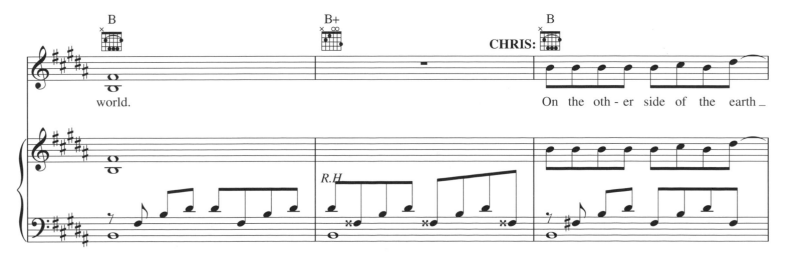

world.　CHRIS:　On the oth - er side of the earth _

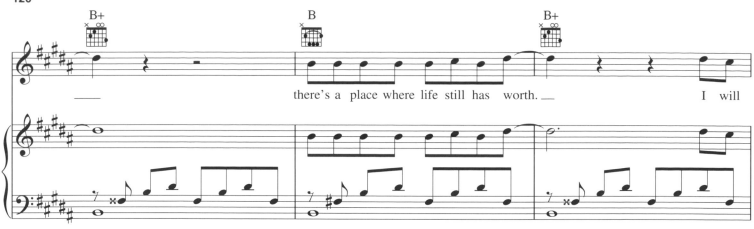

there's a place where life still has worth. __ I will

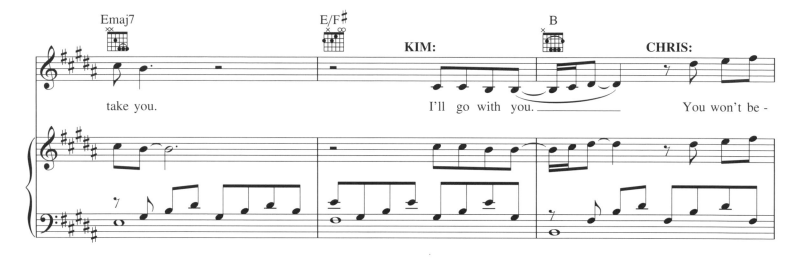

take you. KIM: I'll go with you. _____ CHRIS: You won't be -

lieve all the things you'll see. ___ I know 'cause you'll see them all with me. __

CHRIS:
KIM:
If we're to - geth - er, well then, we'll hear it a - gain, a

rit.

song played on a so - lo sax - o - phone,

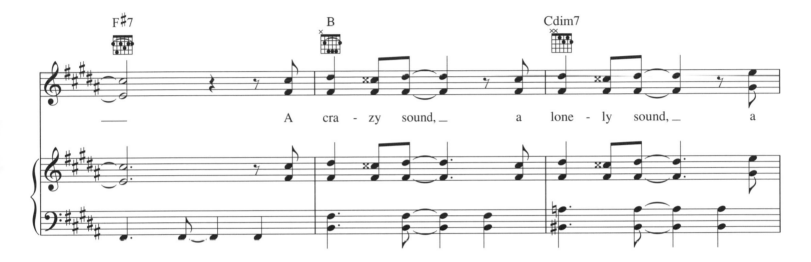

A cra - zy sound, a lone - ly sound, a

cry that tells us love goes on and on.

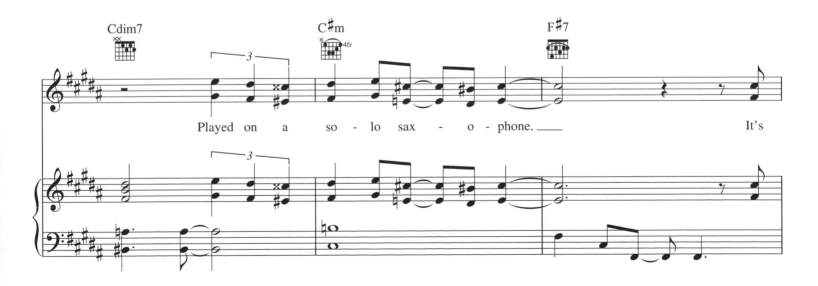

Played on a so - lo sax - o - phone. It's

122

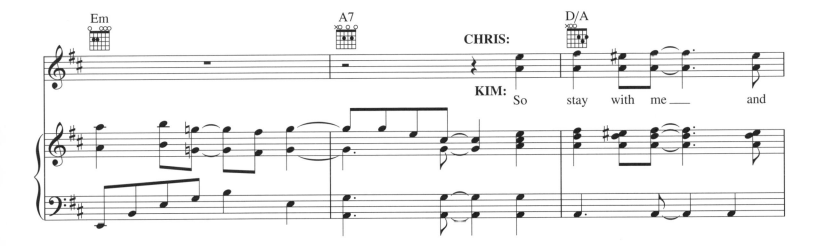

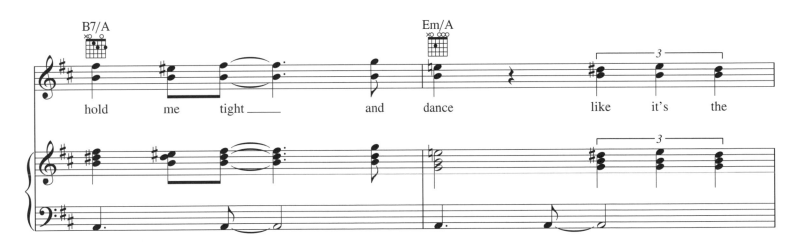

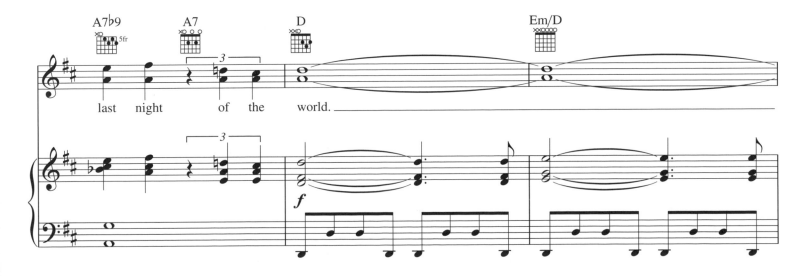

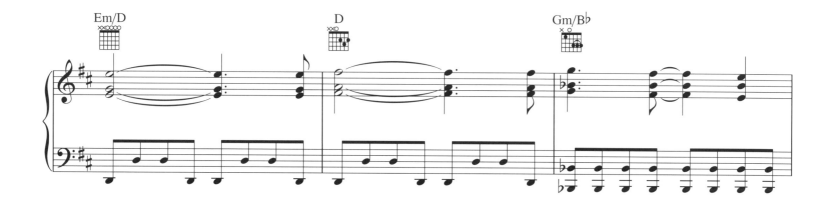

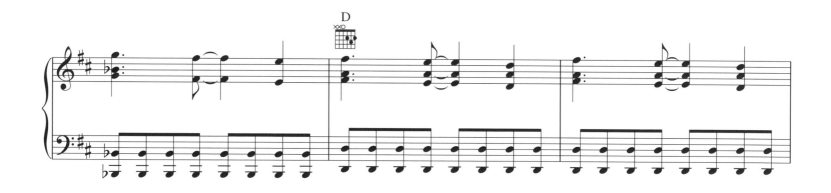

LOOK TO THE RAINBOW
from FINIAN'S RAINBOW

Words by E.Y. "YIP" HARBURG
Music by BURTON LANE

127

MAME
from MAME

Music and Lyric by
JERRY HERMAN

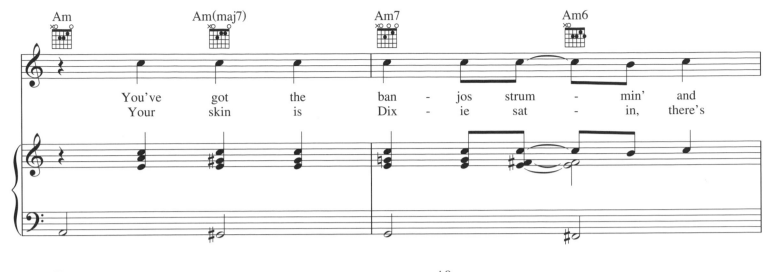

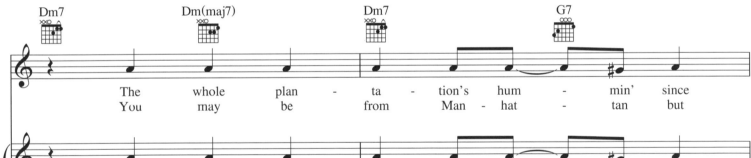

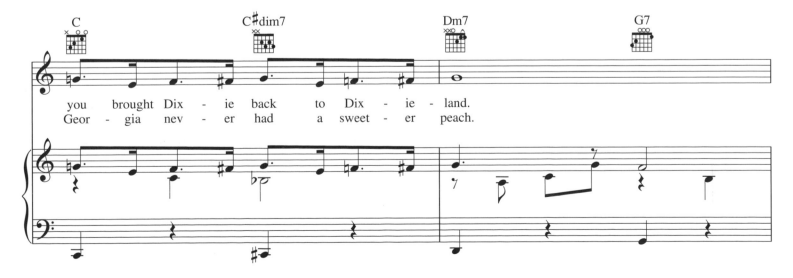

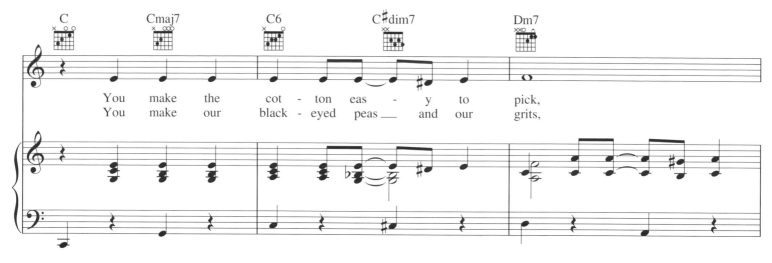

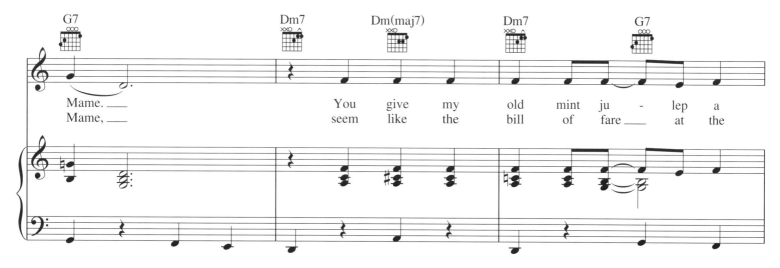

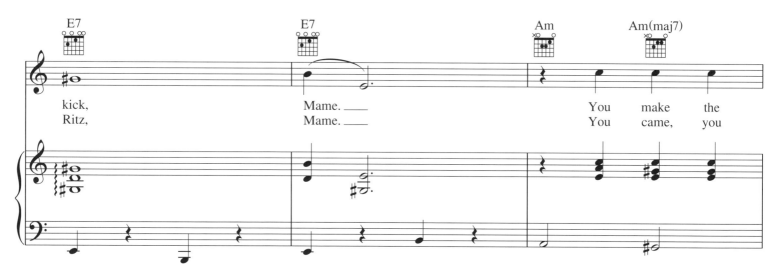

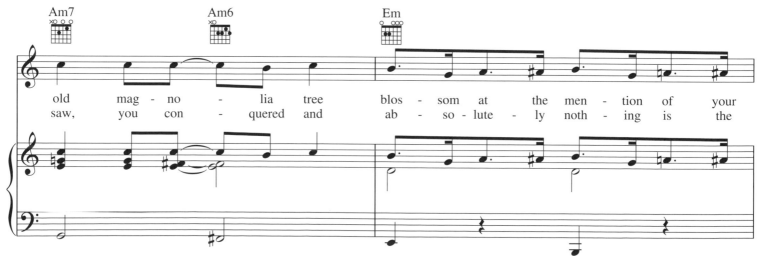

MEMORY
from CATS

Music by ANDREW LLOYD WEBBER
Text by TREVOR NUNN after T.S. ELIOT

GRIZABELLA:

Mid - night. _____ Not a sound from the pave - ment. _____ Has the moon lost her
Mem - ory _____ all a - lone in the moon - light _____ I can smile at the

mem - ory? _____ She is smil-ing a - lone. _____ In the
old days, _____ I was beau-ti-ful then. _____ I re-

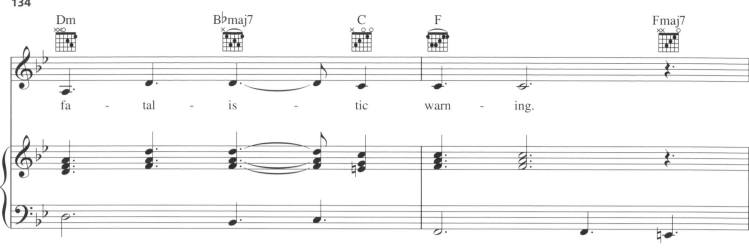

fa - tal - is - tic warn - ing.

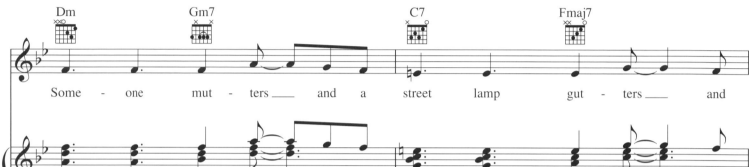

Some - one mut - ters ____ and a street lamp gut - ters ____ and

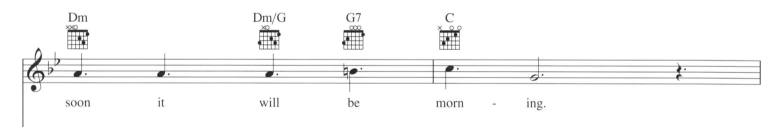

soon it will be morn - ing.

rit.

Day - light. ____ I must wait for the sun - rise, ____ I must think of a

a tempo

new life _____ and I must-n't give in. _____ When the

dawn comes to - night will be a mem - o - ry too _____ and a

new day _____ will be - gin.

136

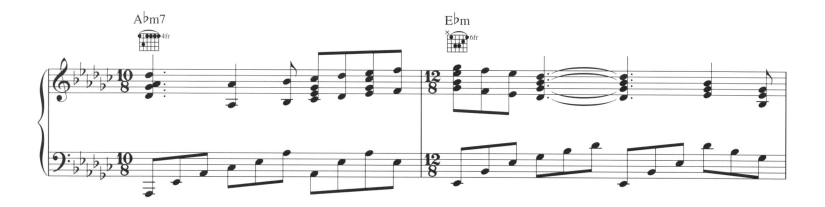

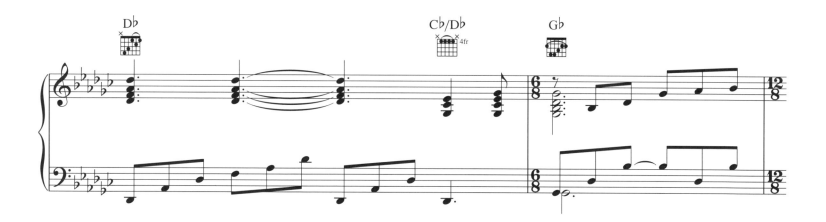

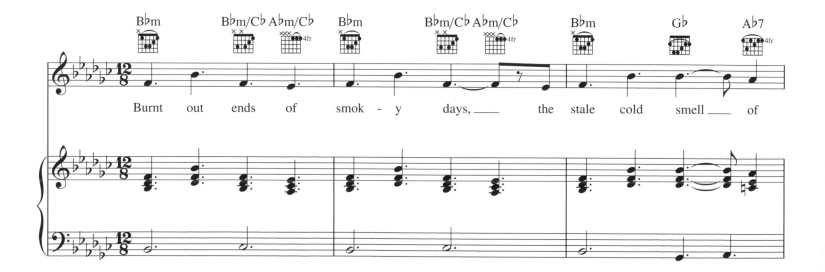

Burnt out ends of smok-y days,___ the stale cold smell___ of

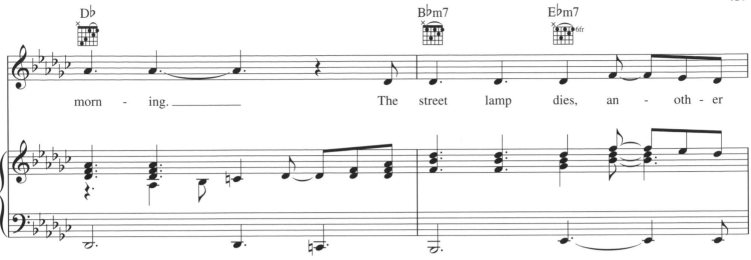

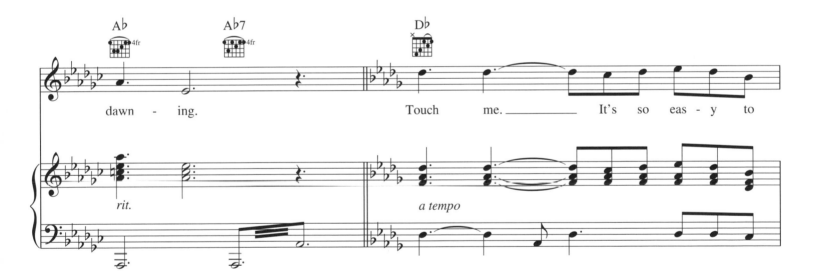

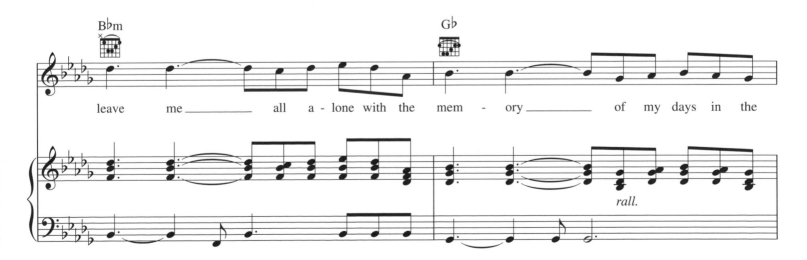

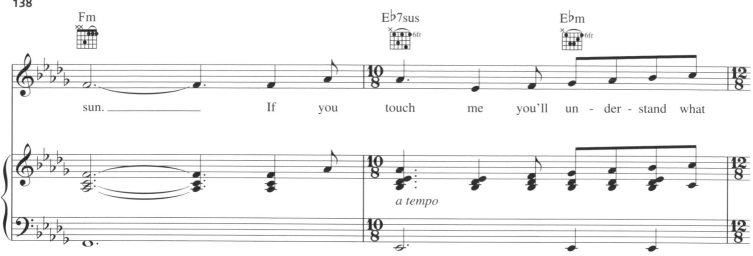

sun. _____ If you touch me you'll un-der-stand what

a tempo

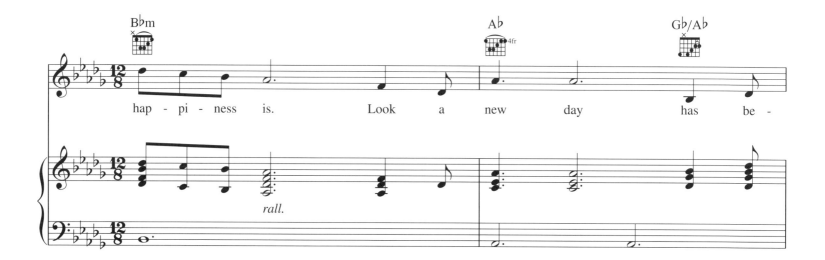

hap - pi - ness is. Look a new day has be -

rall.

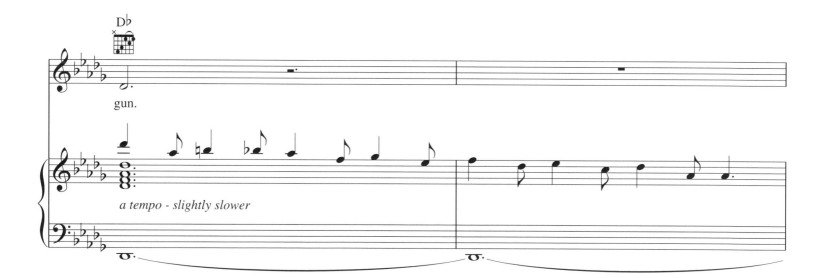

gun.

a tempo - slightly slower

MY FUNNY VALENTINE

from BABES IN ARMS

Words by LORENZ HART
Music by RICHARD RODGERS

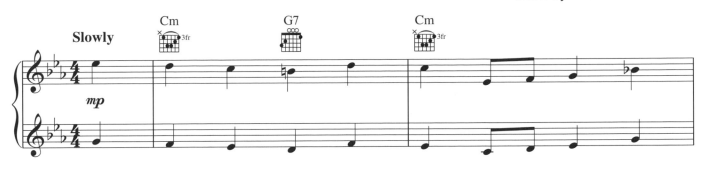

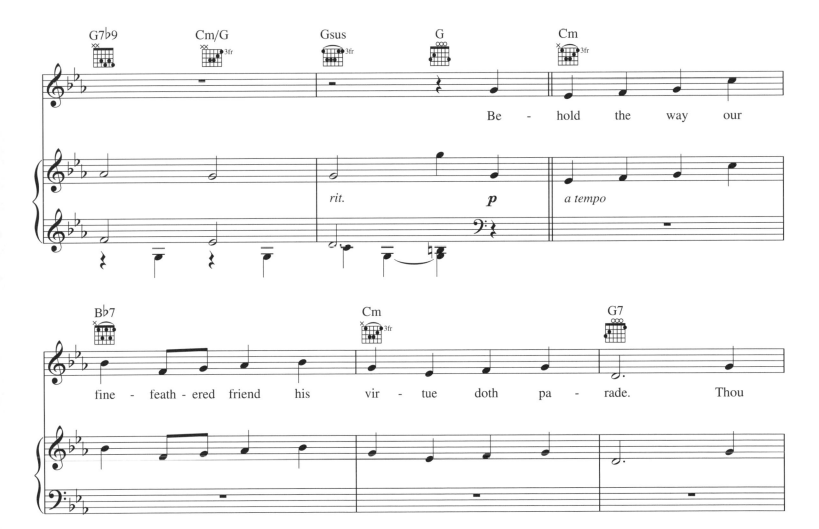

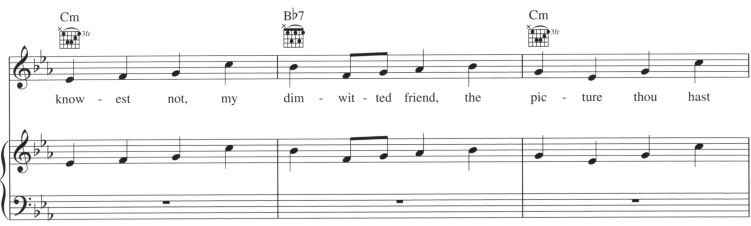

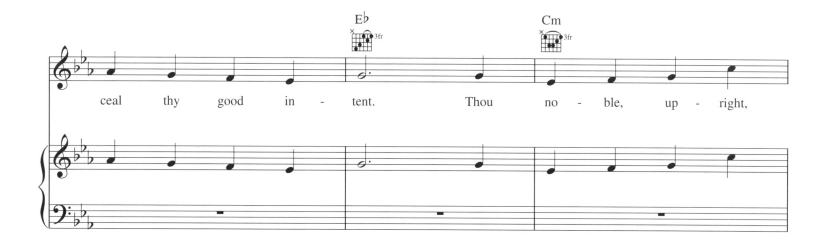

made. Thy va - cant brow and thy tous - led hair con -

ceal thy good in - tent. Thou no - ble, up - right,

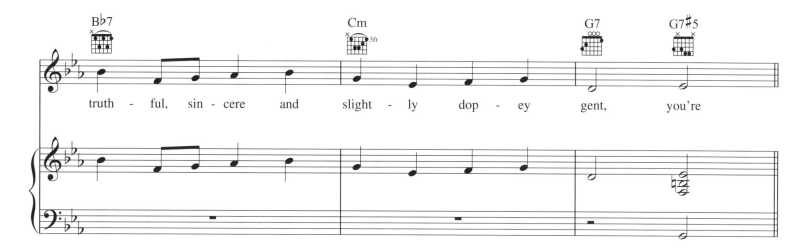

truth - ful, sin - cere and slight - ly dop - ey gent, you're

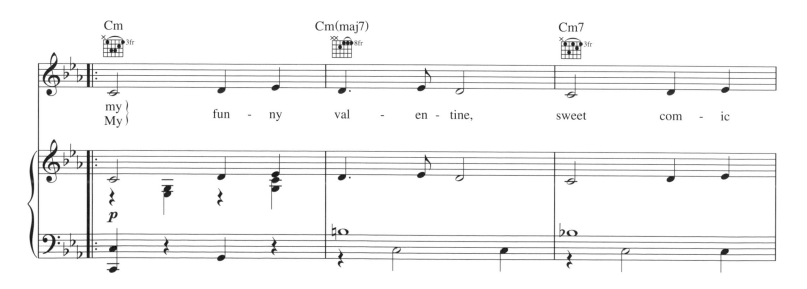

my
My
}
fun - ny val - en - tine, sweet com - ic

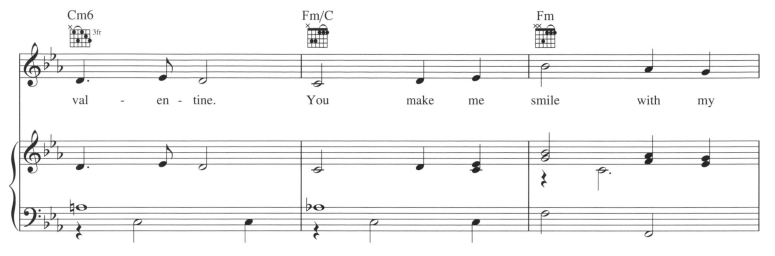

val - en - tine. You make me smile with my

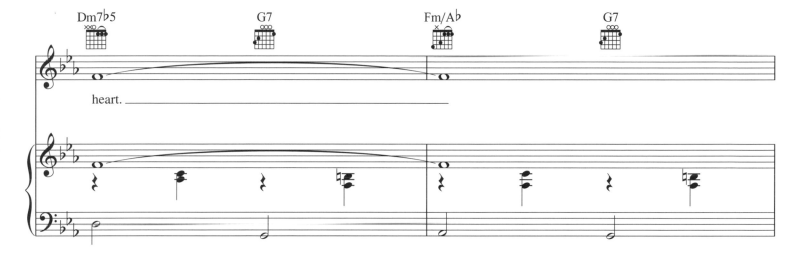

heart.

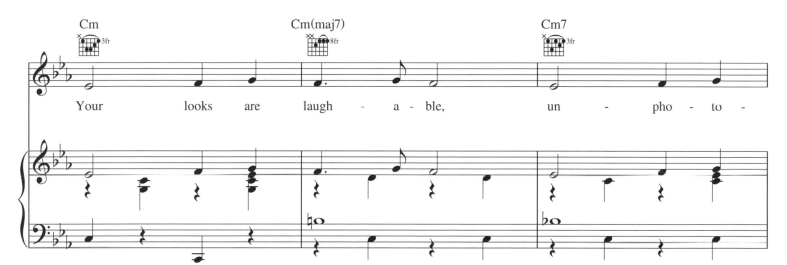

Your looks are laugh - a - ble, un - pho - to -

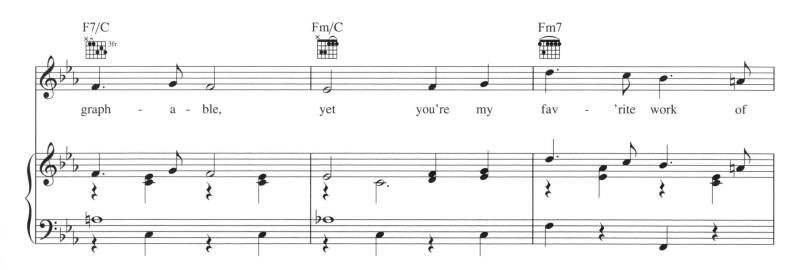

graph - a - ble, yet you're my fav - 'rite work of

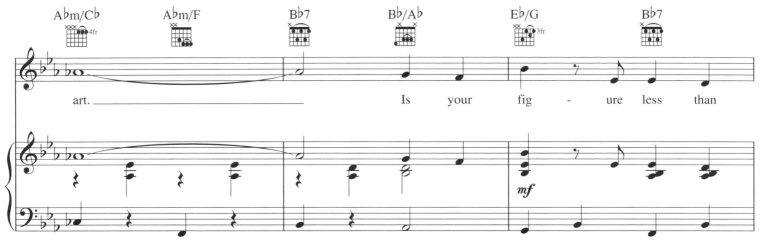

art. _____ Is your fig - ure less than

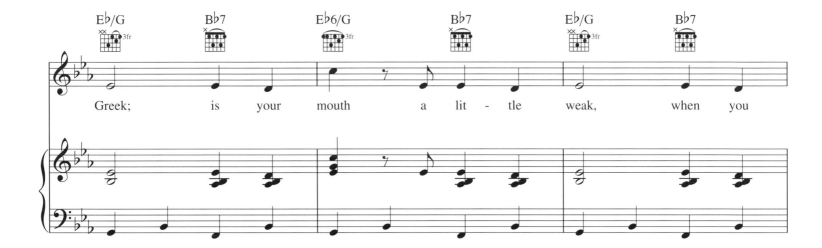

Greek; is your mouth a lit - tle weak, when you

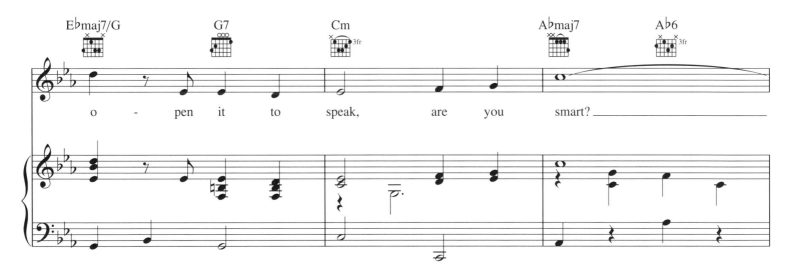

o - pen it to speak, are you smart? _____

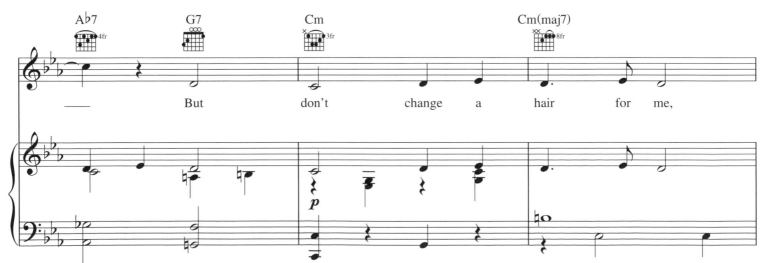

_____ But don't change a hair for me,

THE MOST BEAUTIFUL GIRL IN THE WORLD

from JUMBO

Words by LORENZ HART
Music by RICHARD RODGERS

Moderate Waltz tempo

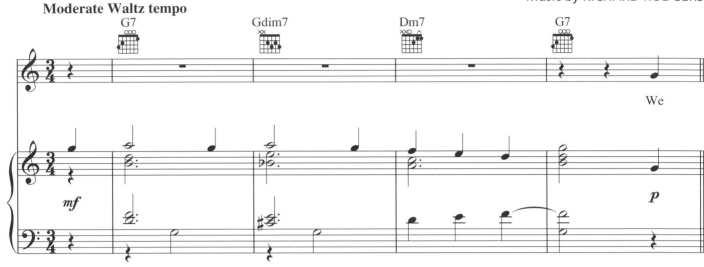

We

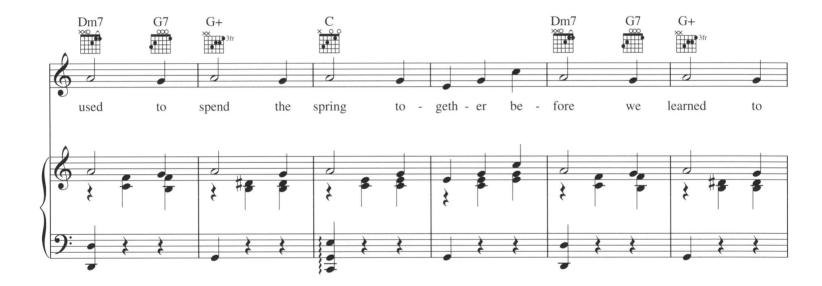

used to spend the spring to-geth-er be-fore we learned to

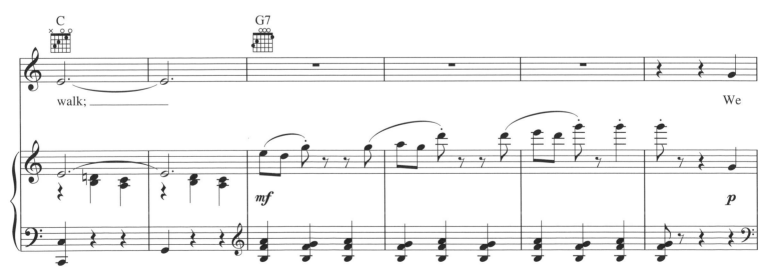

walk; _____ We

145

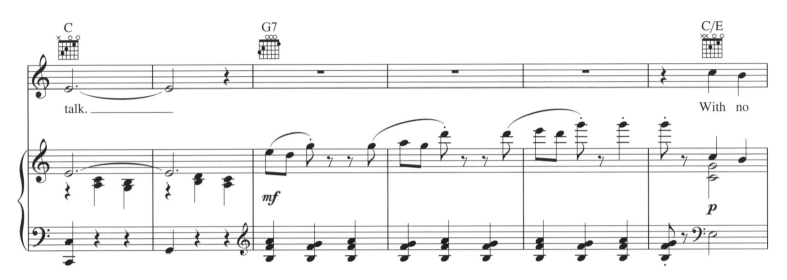

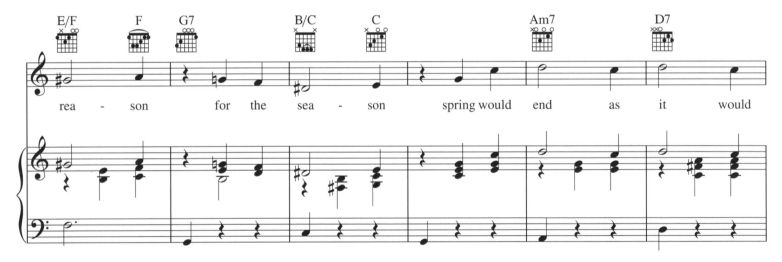

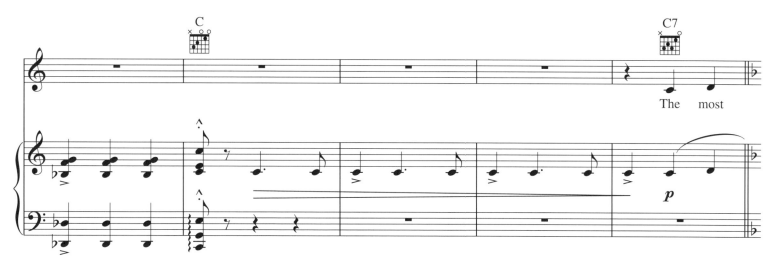

147

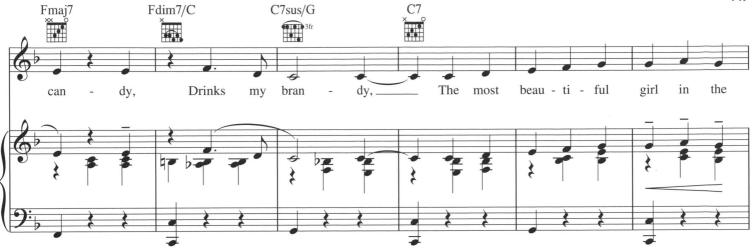

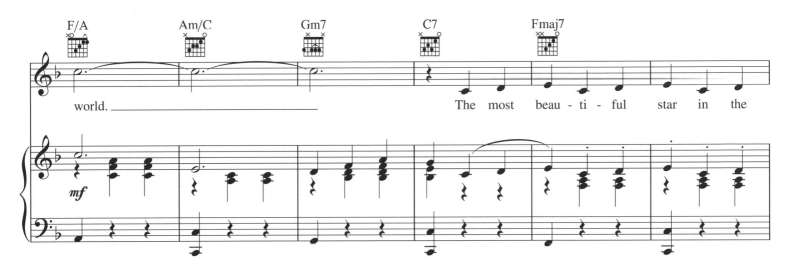

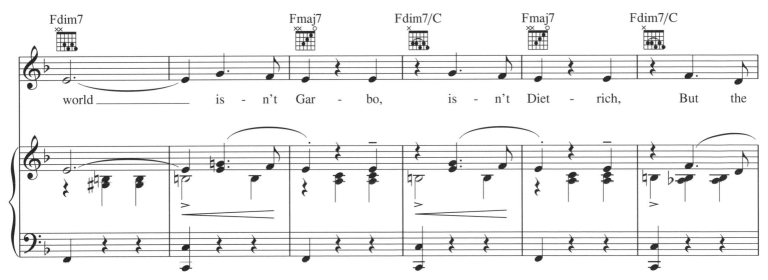

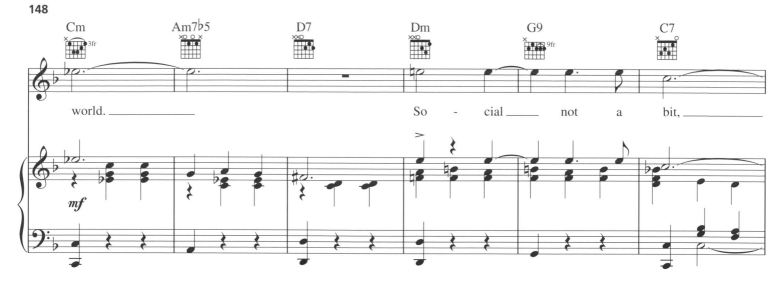

THE MUSIC OF THE NIGHT

from THE PHANTOM OF THE OPERA

Music by ANDREW LLOYD WEBBER
Lyrics by CHARLES HART
Additional Lyrics by RICHARD STILGOE

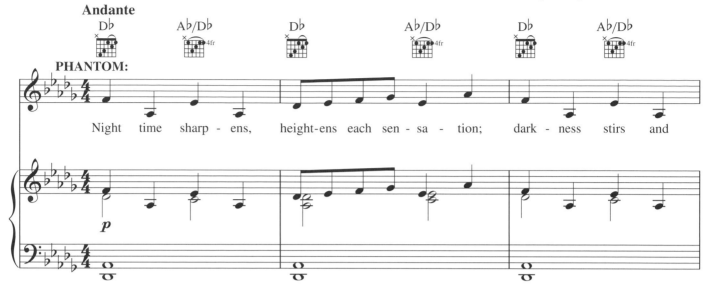

PHANTOM:

Night time sharp-ens, height-ens each sen-sa - tion; dark - ness stirs and

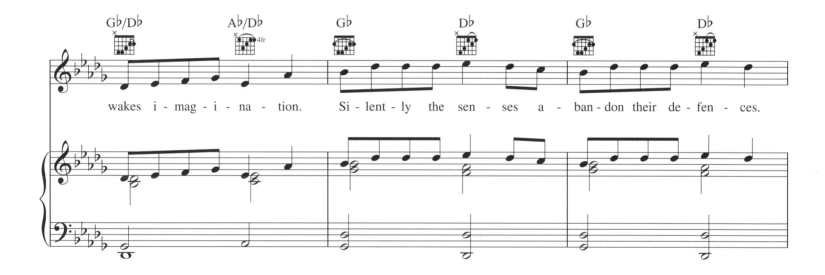

wakes i-mag - i - na - tion. Si - lent-ly the sen - ses a - ban-don their de - fen - ces.

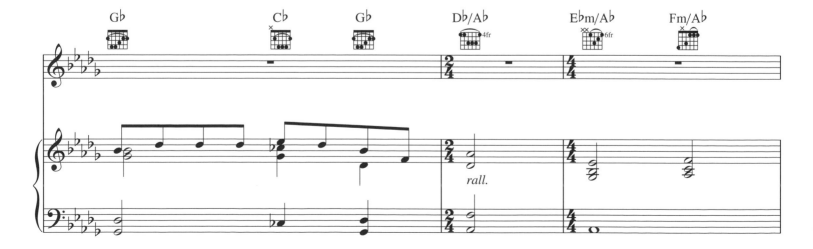

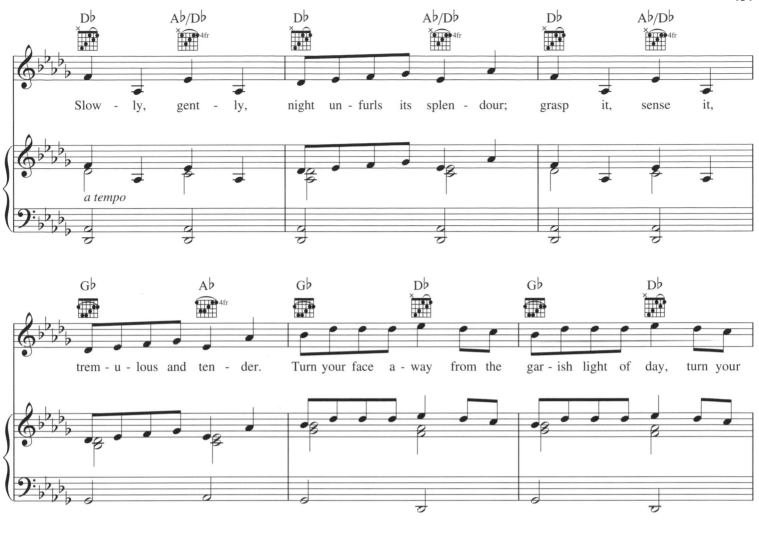

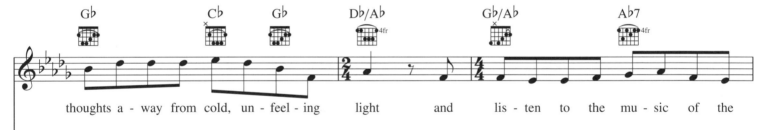

Float - ing, fall - ing, sweet in - tox - i - ca - tion. Touch me, trust me,

sa - vour each sen - sa - tion. Let the dream be - gin, let your dark - er side give in to the

pow - er of the mu - sic that I write, the pow - er of the mu - sic of the

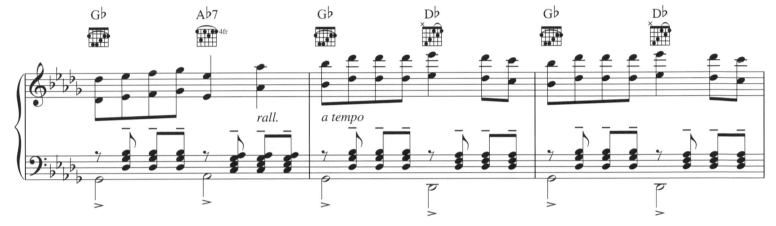

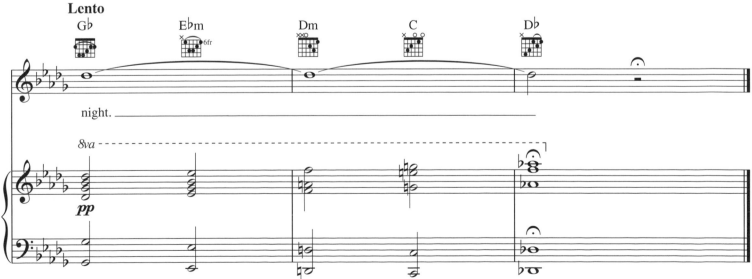

MY FAVORITE THINGS
from THE SOUND OF MUSIC

Lyrics by OSCAR HAMMERSTEIN II
Music by RICHARD RODGERS

OH, WHAT A BEAUTIFUL MORNIN'

from OKLAHOMA!

Lyrics by OSCAR HAMMERSTEIN II
Music by RICHARD RODGERS

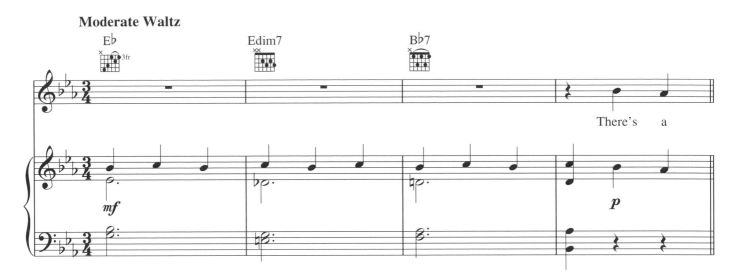

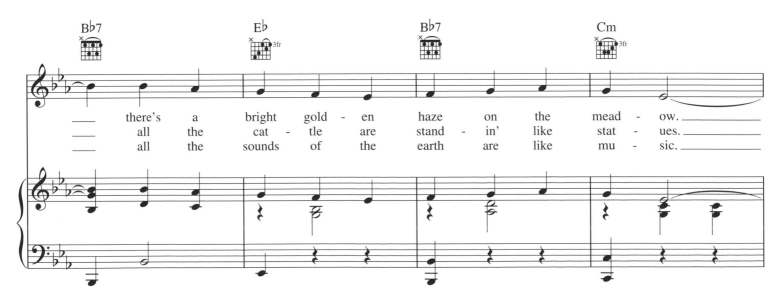

161

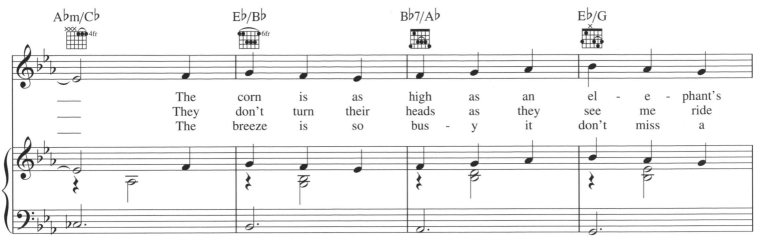

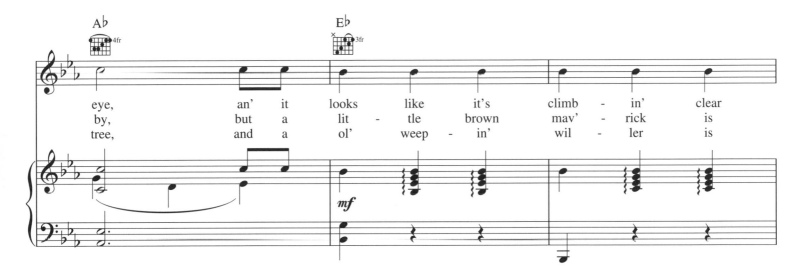

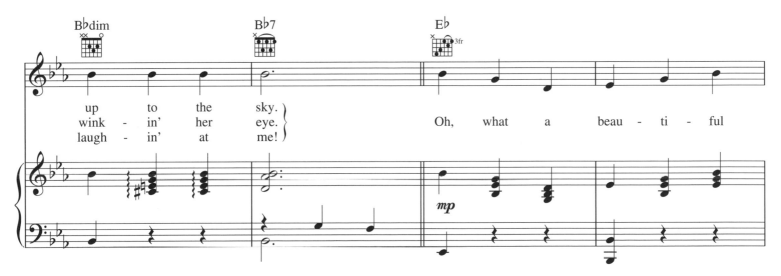

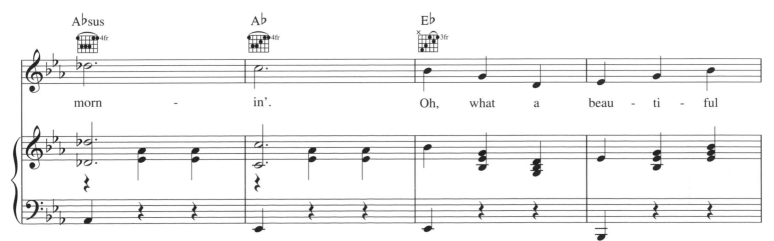

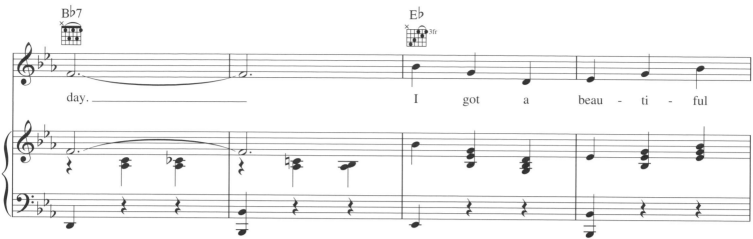

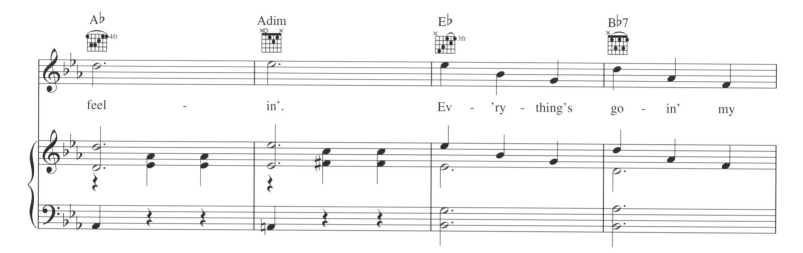

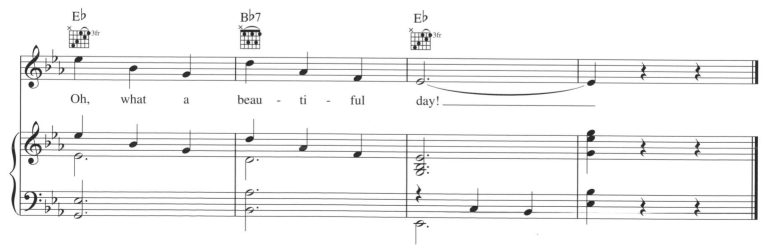

OL' MAN RIVER

from SHOW BOAT

Lyrics by OSCAR HAMMERSTEIN II
Music by JEROME KERN

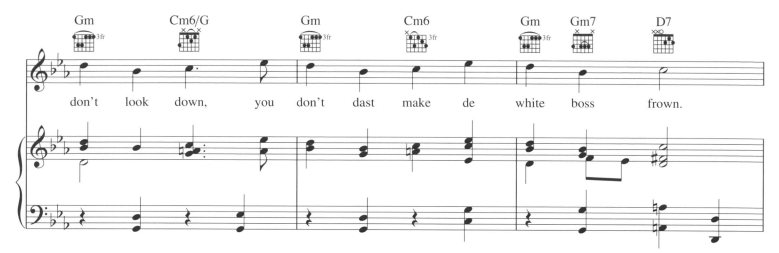

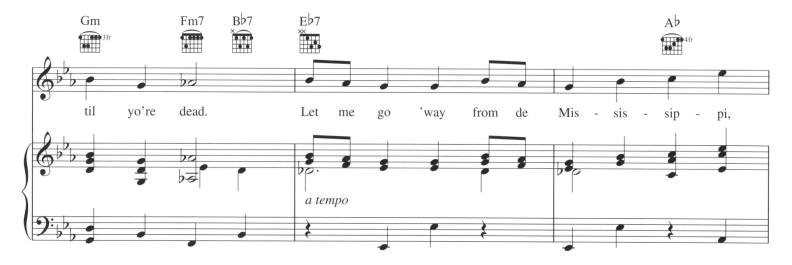

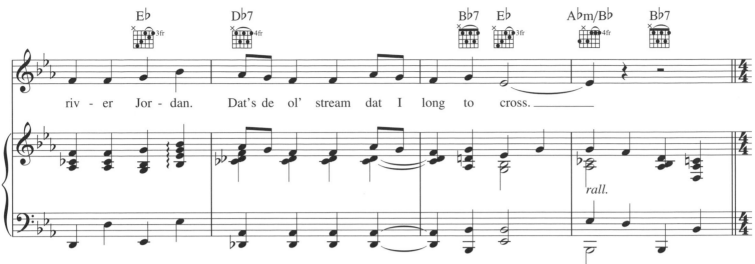

riv - er Jor - dan. Dat's de ol' stream dat I long to cross. _____

rall.

Slower

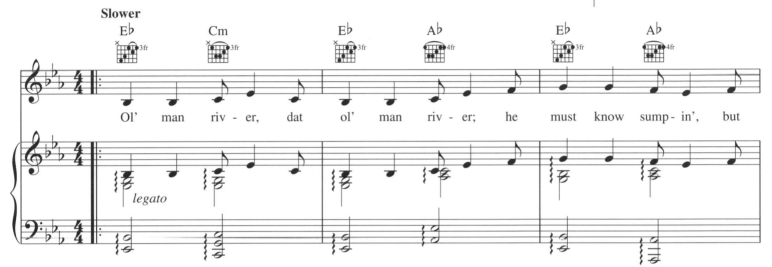

Ol' man riv - er, dat ol' man riv - er; he must know sump - in', but

legato

don't say noth - in'. He jus' keeps roll - in', he keeps on roll - in' a -

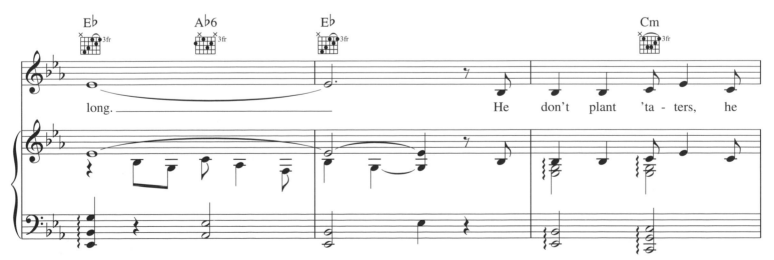

long. _____ He don't plant 'ta - ters, he

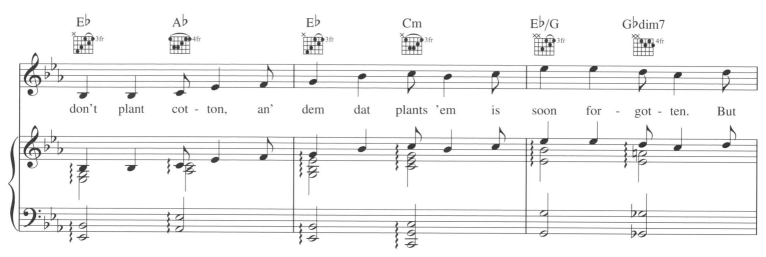

don't plant cot-ton, an' dem dat plants 'em is soon for-got-ten. But

ol' man riv-er, he jus' keeps roll-in' a - long. _____

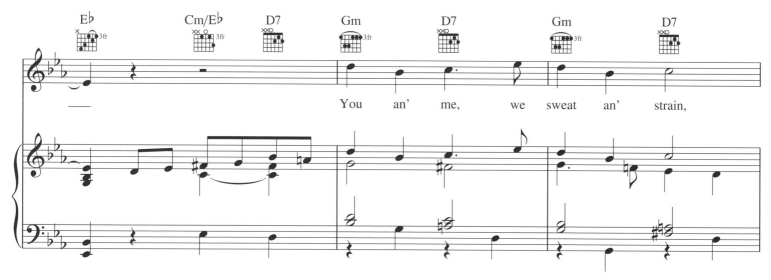

_____ You an' me, we sweat an' strain,

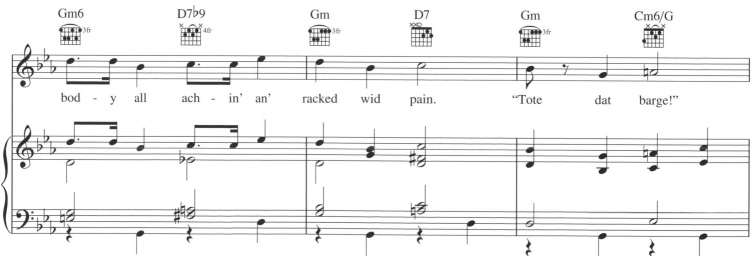

bod - y all ach - in' an' racked wid pain. "Tote dat barge!"

167

"Lift dat bale," Git a lit - tle drunk an' you land in jail.

Ah gits wea - ry an' sick of try - in'. Ah'm tired of liv - in' an'

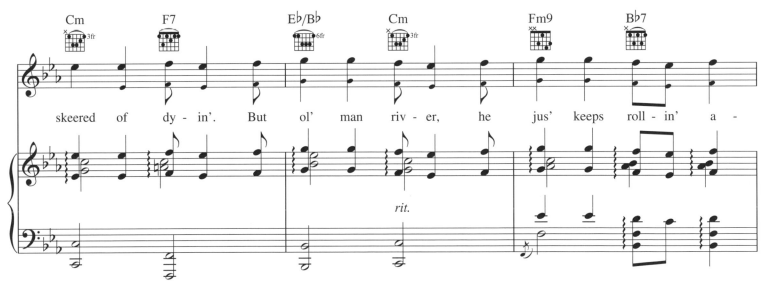

skeered of dy - in'. But ol' man riv - er, he jus' keeps roll - in' a-

rit.

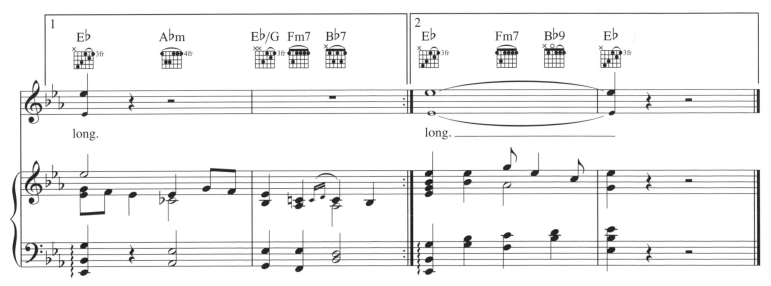

long.   long.

ON A CLEAR DAY
(You Can See Forever)
from ON A CLEAR DAY YOU CAN SEE FOREVER

Words by ALAN JAY LERNER
Music by BURTON LANE

169

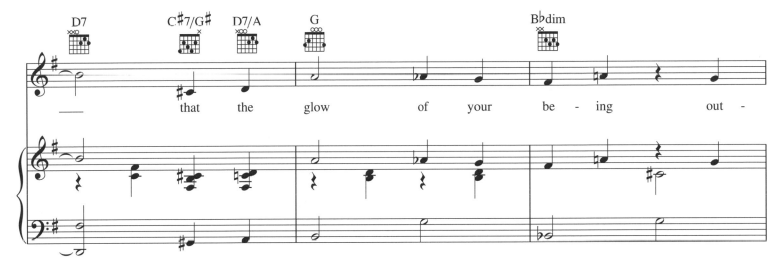

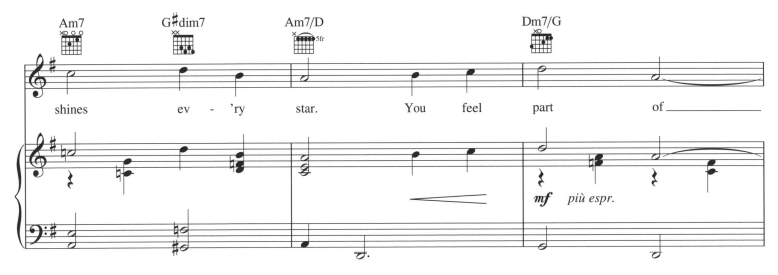

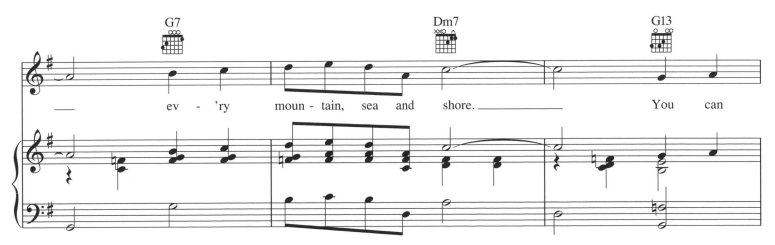

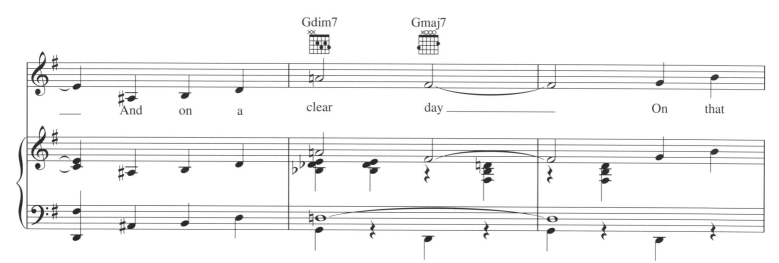

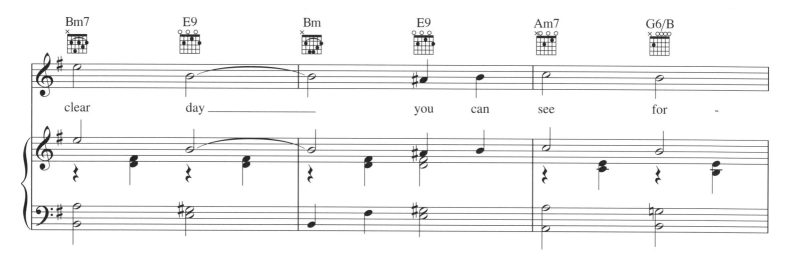

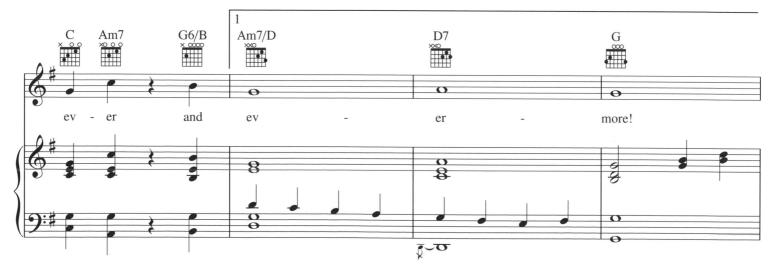

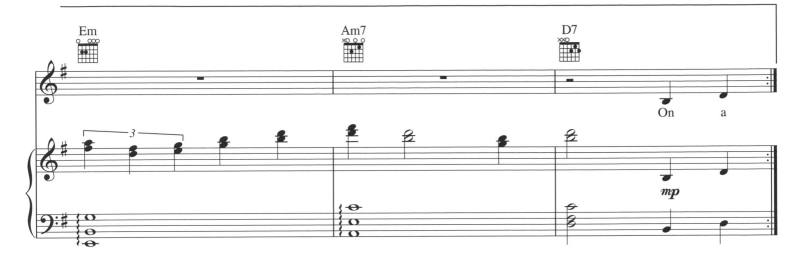

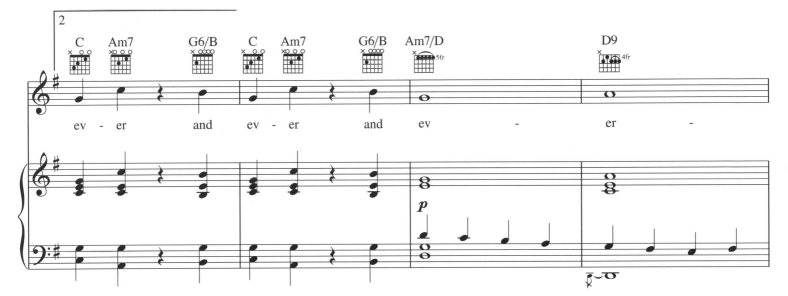

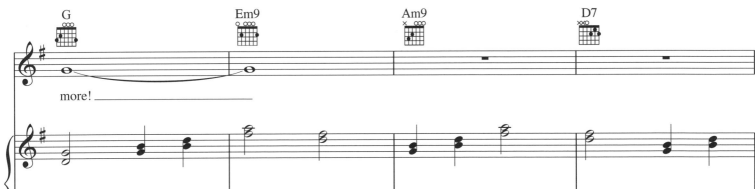

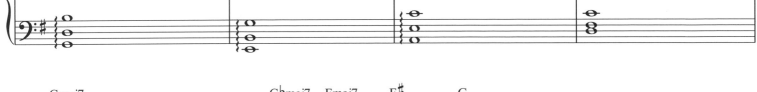

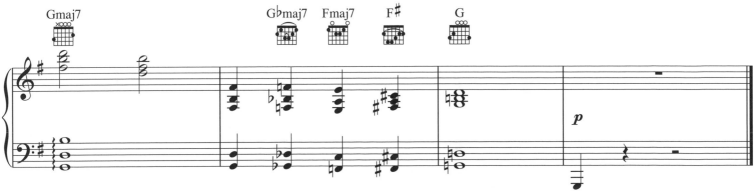

ON THE STREET WHERE YOU LIVE

from MY FAIR LADY

Words by ALAN JAY LERNER
Music by FREDERICK LOEWE

173

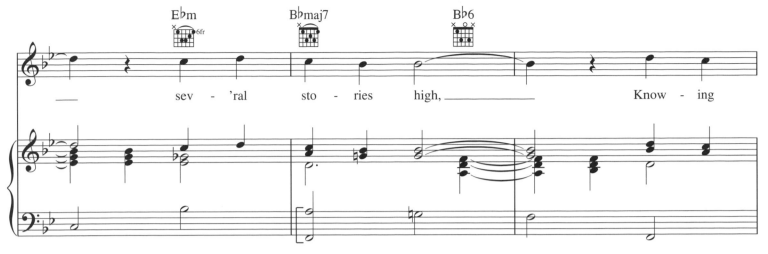

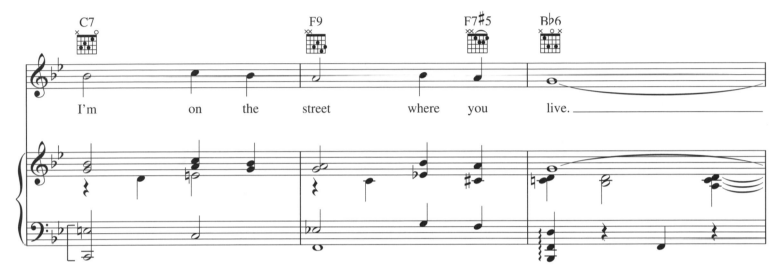

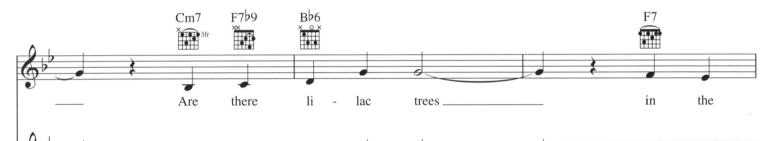

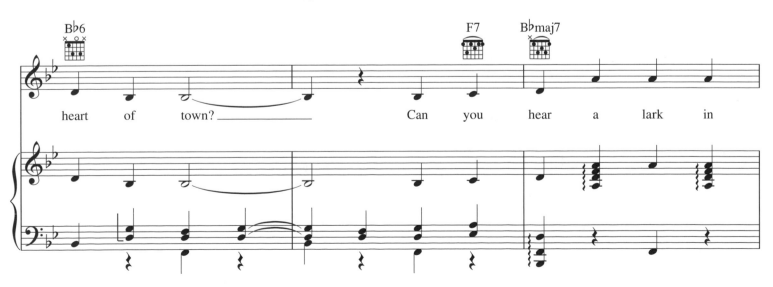

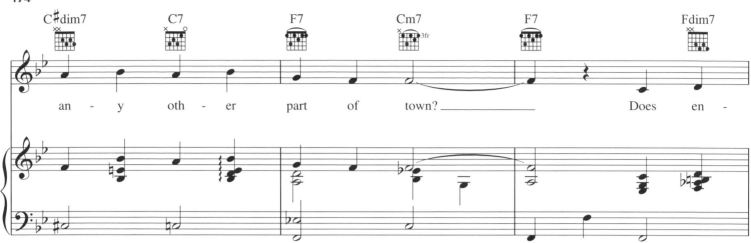

an - y oth - er part of town? _____ Does en -

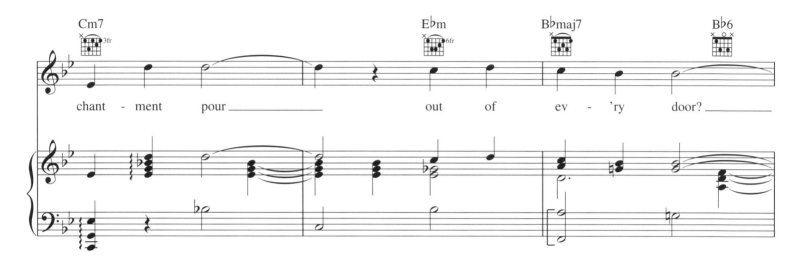

chant - ment pour _____ out of ev - 'ry door? _____

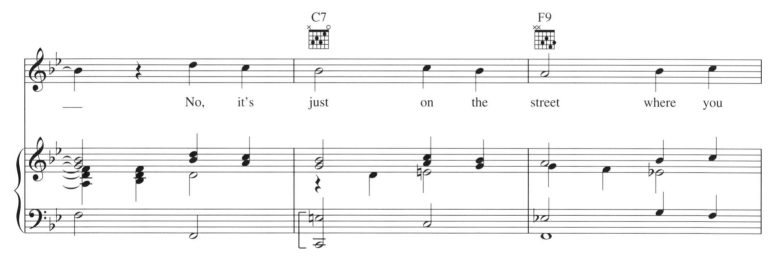

___ No, it's just on the street where you

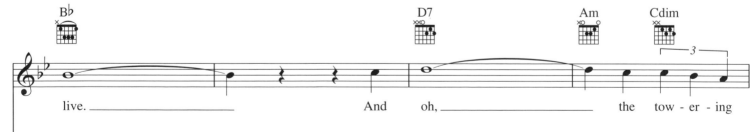

live. _____ And oh, _____ the tow - er - ing

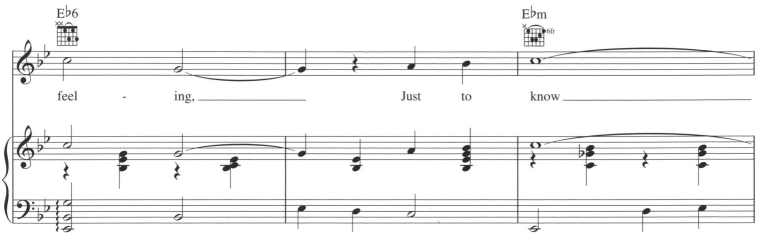

feel - ing, _____ Just to know _____

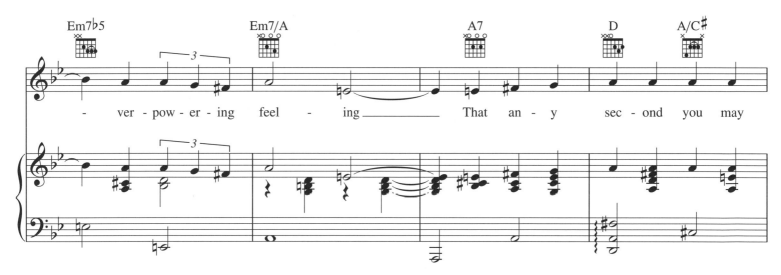

___ some - how you are near! _____ The o -

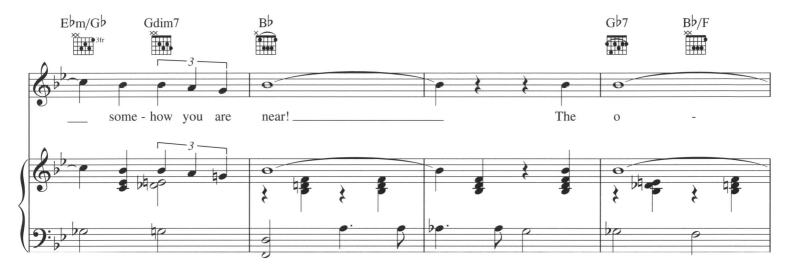

- ver - pow - er - ing feel - ing _____ That an - y sec - ond you may

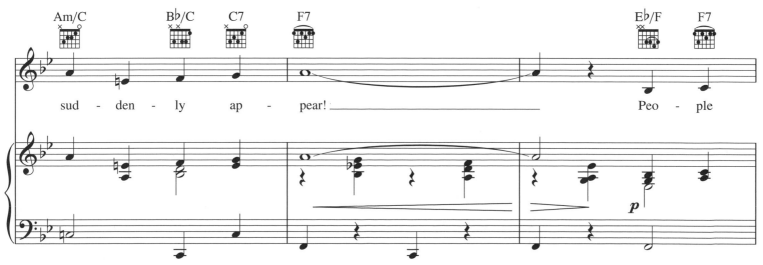

sud - den - ly ap - pear! _____ Peo - ple

POPULAR
from the Broadway Musical WICKED

Music and Lyrics by
STEPHEN SCHWARTZ

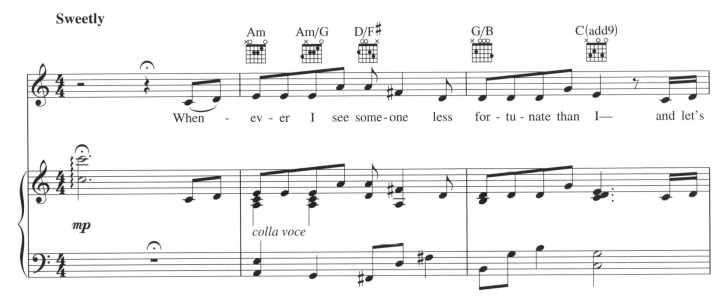

When - ev - er I see some-one less for - tu - nate than I— and let's

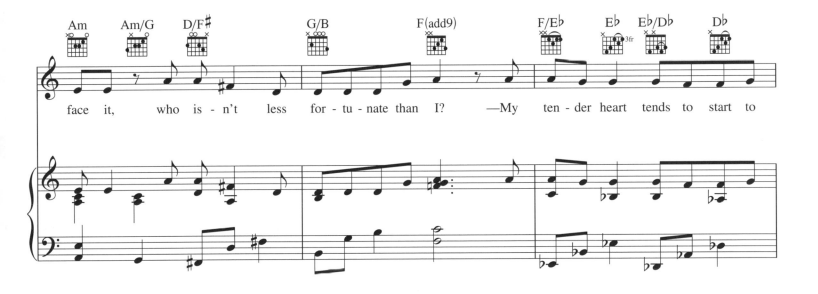

face it, who is - n't less for - tu - nate than I? —My ten - der heart tends to start to

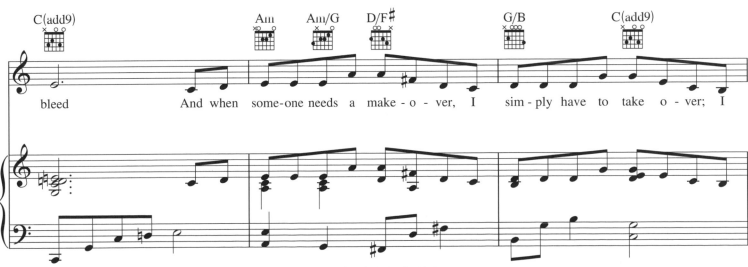

bleed   And when some-one needs a make - o - ver, I sim - ply have to take o - ver; I

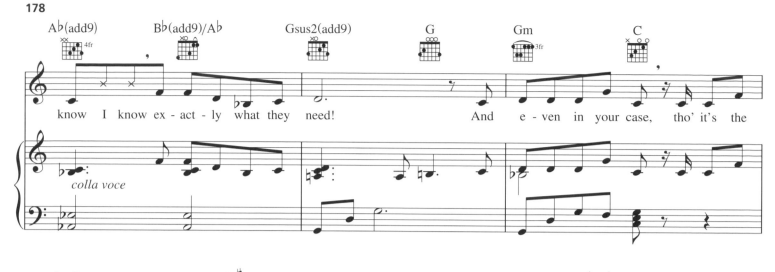

know I know ex - act - ly what they need! And e - ven in your case, tho' it's the

tough - est case I've yet to face, ___ don't wor - ry, I'm de - ter - mined to suc -

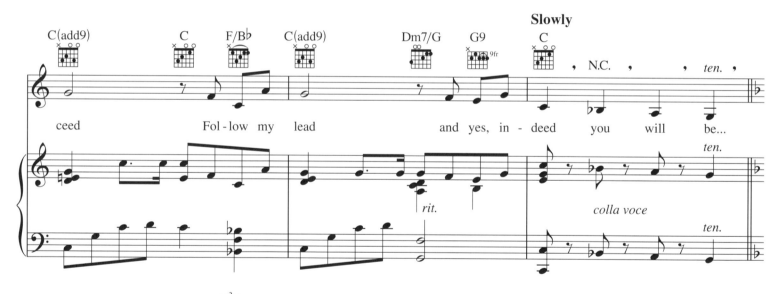

ceed Fol - low my lead and yes, in - deed you will be...

Pop - u - lar, ___ You're gon - na be pop - u - lar! I'll teach ___ you the

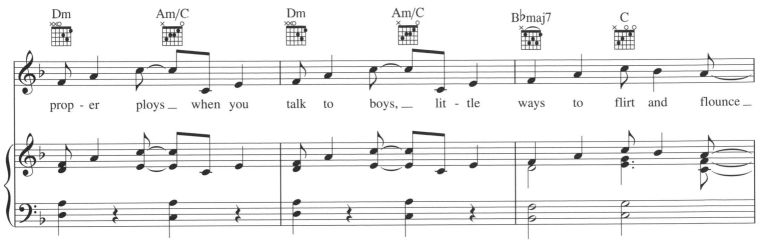

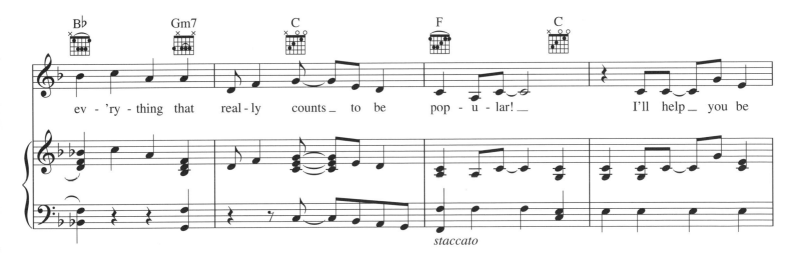

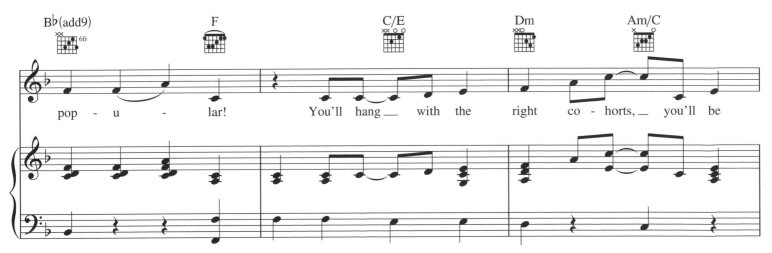

good at sports, ___ know the slang you've got to know ___ So let's

start, 'cause you've got an aw - f'lly long ___ way to go! ___

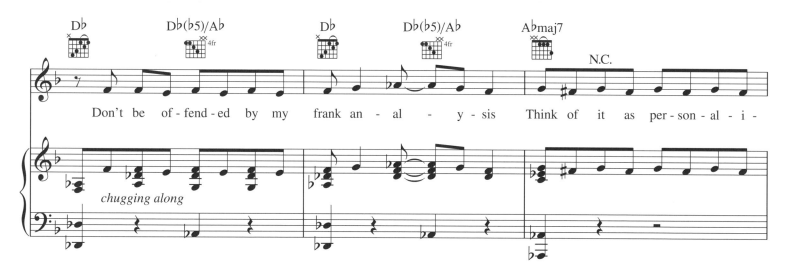

Don't be of - fend - ed by my frank an - al - y - sis Think of it as per - son - al - i -

chugging along

ty di - al - y - sis Now that I've cho - sen to be - come a pal, ___ a sis -

-ter and ad - vis - er, there's __ no - bod - y wis - er, not __ when it comes __ to

pop - u - lar __ I know __ a - bout pop - u - lar!

And with __ an as - sist from me __ to be who you'll be, __ in -

stead of drear - y who - you - were... __ are... There's noth - ing that can stop you from __

Gm7　C　F　N.C.

be - com - ing pop - u - ler... lar... _____

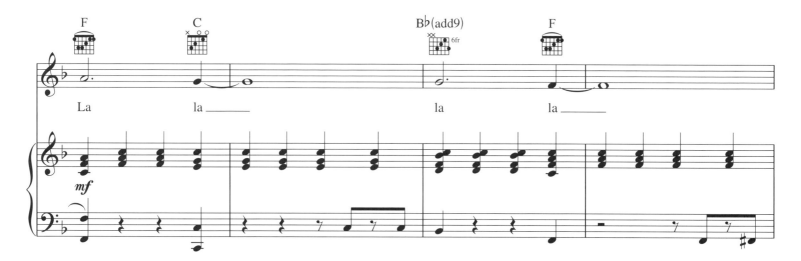

F　C　B♭(add9)　F

La la _____ la la _____

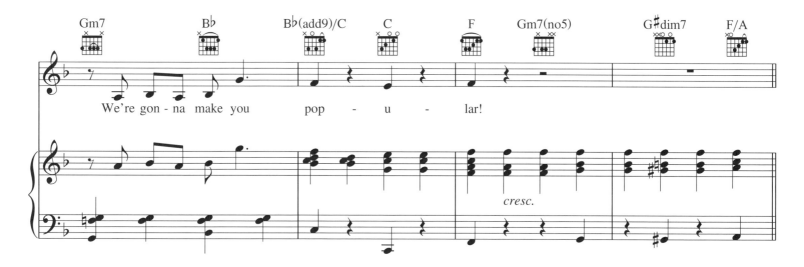

Gm7　B♭　B♭(add9)/C　C　F　Gm7(no5)　G♯dim7　F/A

We're gon - na make you pop - u - lar!

cresc.

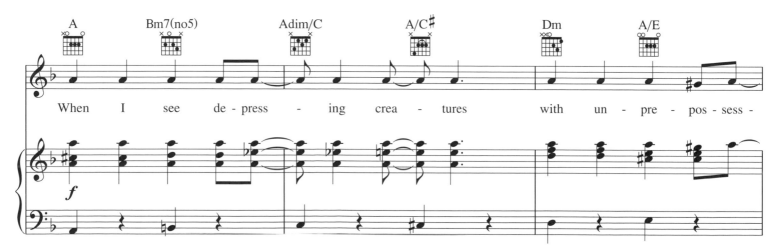

A　Bm7(no5)　Adim/C　A/C♯　Dm　A/E

When I see de - press - ing crea - tures with un - pre - pos - sess -

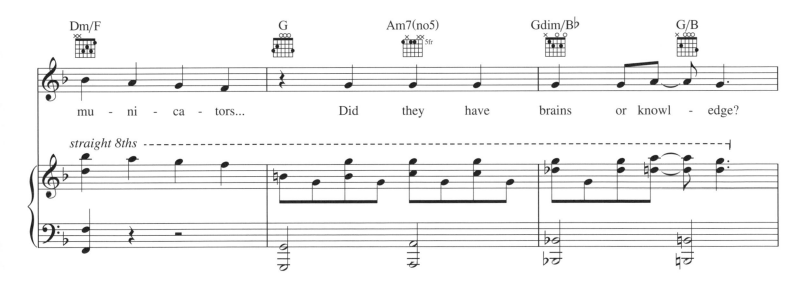

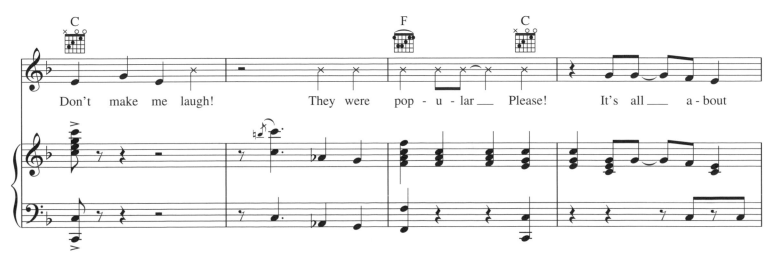

pop - u - lar! It's not _ a - bout ap - ti - tude, _ it's the

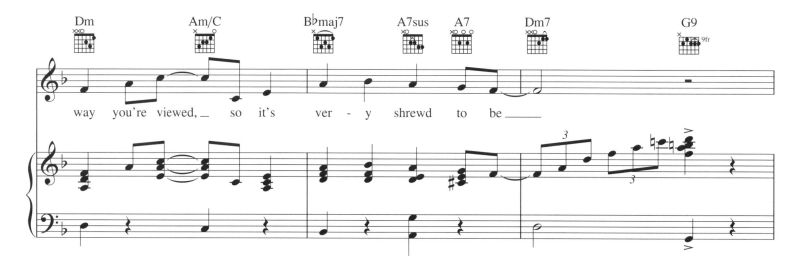

way you're viewed, _ so it's ver - y shrewd to be _

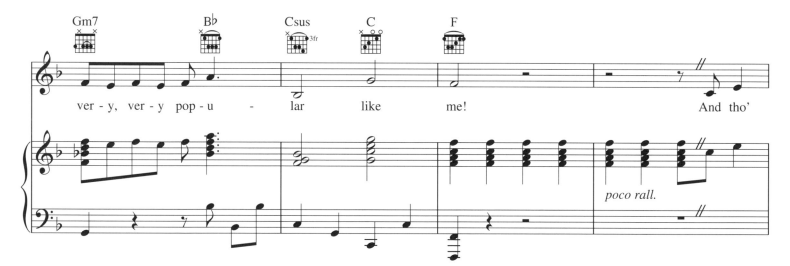

ver - y, ver - y pop - u - lar like me! And tho'

Freely

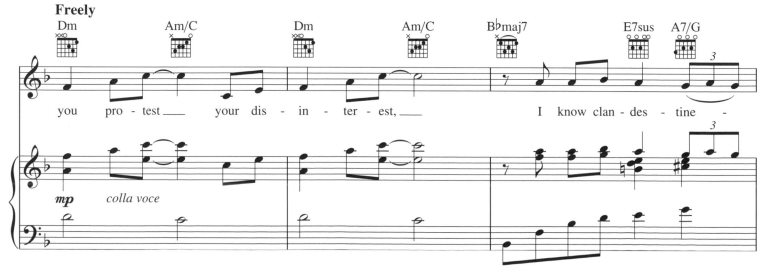

you pro - test _ your dis - in - ter - est, _ I know clan - des - tine -

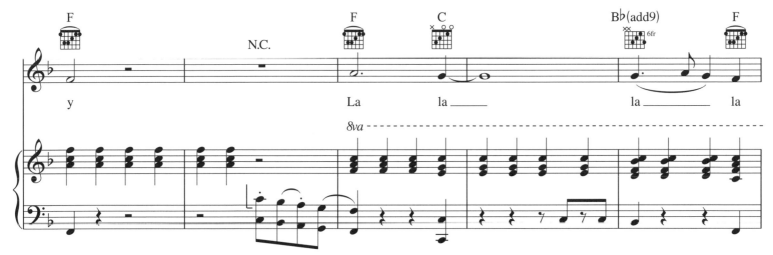

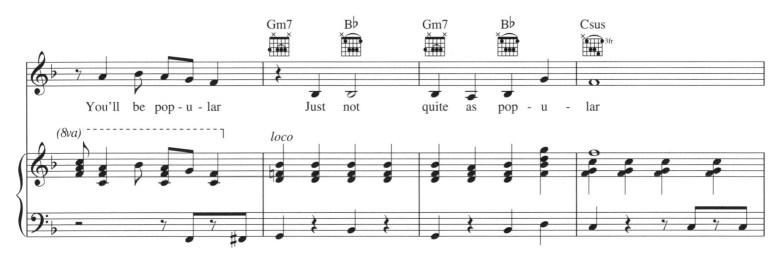

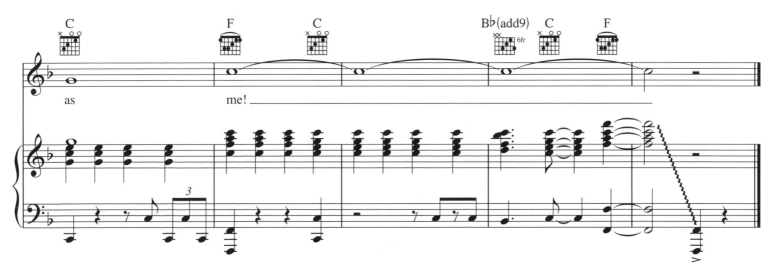

PEOPLE
from FUNNY GIRL

Words by BOB MERRILL
Music by JULE STYNE

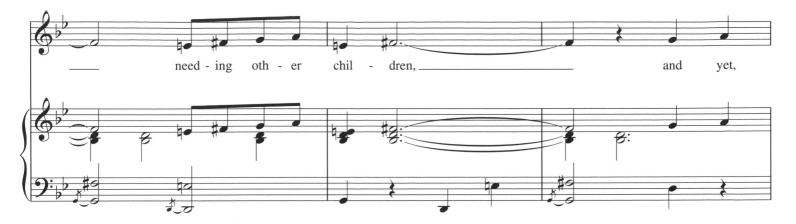

need - ing oth - er chil - dren, _____ and yet,

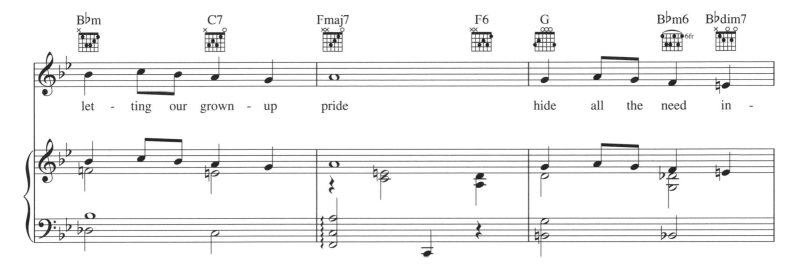

let - ting our grown - up pride hide all the need in -

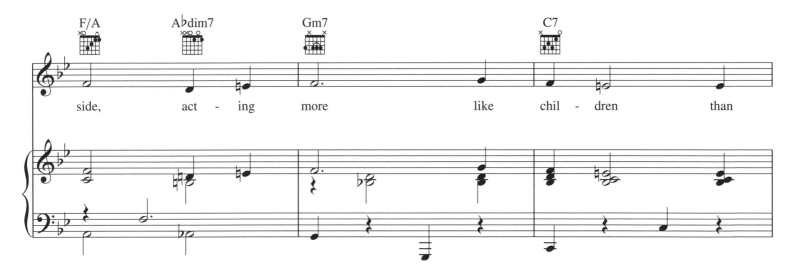

side, act - ing more like chil - dren than

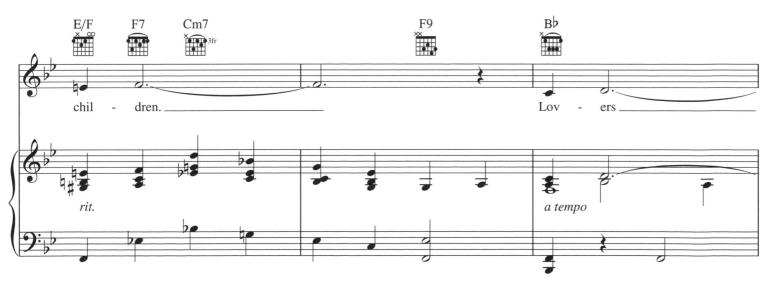

chil - dren. _____ Lov - ers _____

PUT ON A HAPPY FACE

from BYE BYE BIRDIE

Lyric by LEE ADAMS
Music by CHARLES STROUSE

SEASONS OF LOVE

from RENT

Words and Music by
JONATHAN LARSON

Five hun-dred twen-ty-five thou-sand six hun-dred min - utes,

five hun-dred twen-ty-five thou-sand mo-ments so __ dear. __ Five hun-dred twen-ty-five thou-sand

six hun-dred min - utes. How do you meas-ure, meas-ure a __ year? __ In

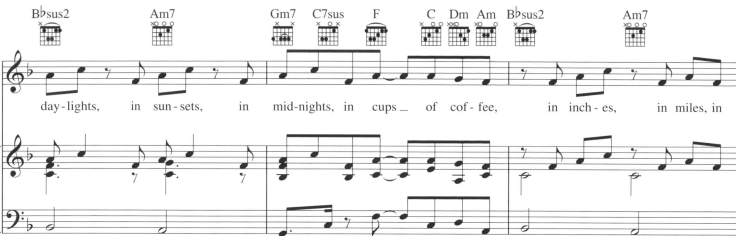

day-lights, in sun-sets, in mid-nights, in cups __ of cof - fee, in inch - es, in miles, in

laugh-ter, in ___ strife, __ in five hun-dred twen-ty-five thou-sand six hun-dred min - utes. How

do you meas-ure a year in ___ the life? __ How a-bout love? _____

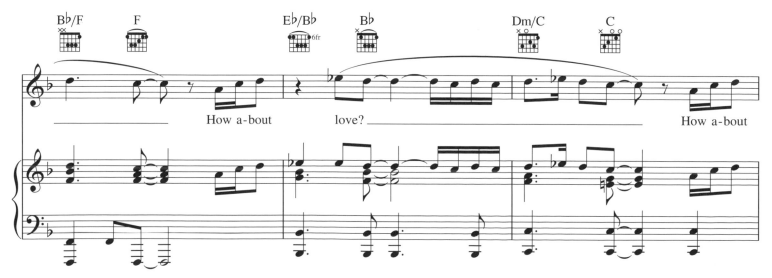

_____ How a-bout love? _____ How a-bout

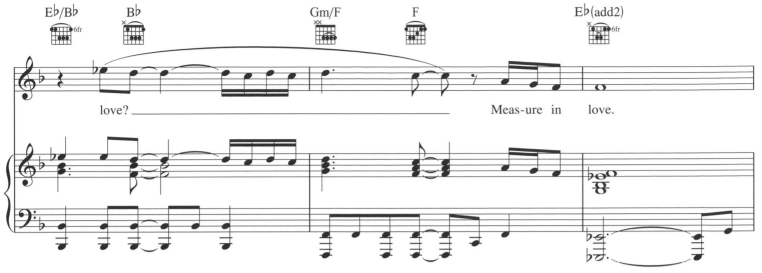

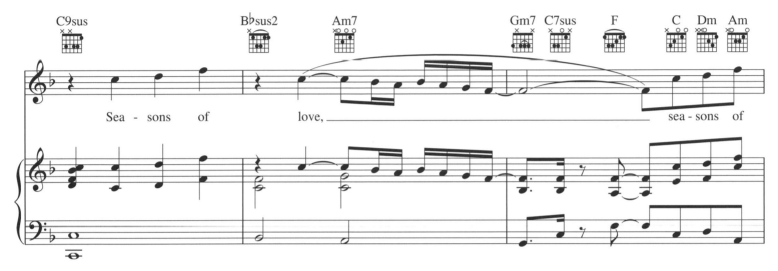

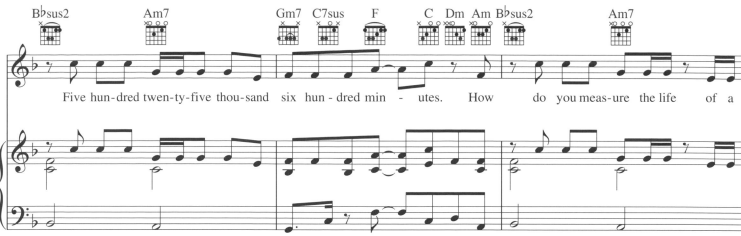

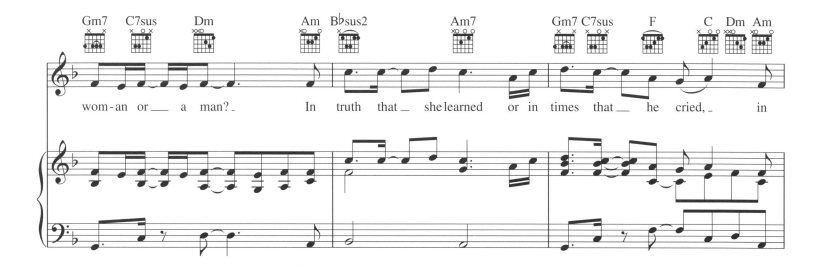

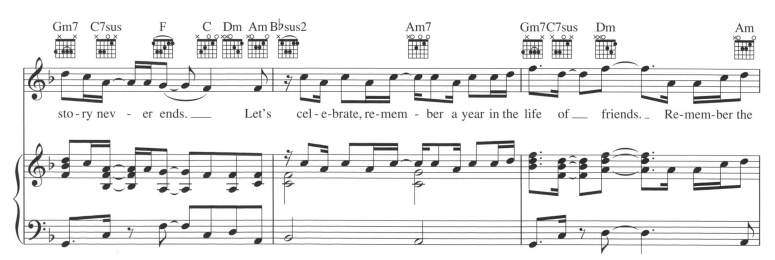

SEPTEMBER SONG
from the Musical Play KNICKERBOCKER HOLIDAY

Words by MAXWELL ANDERSON
Music by KURT WEILL

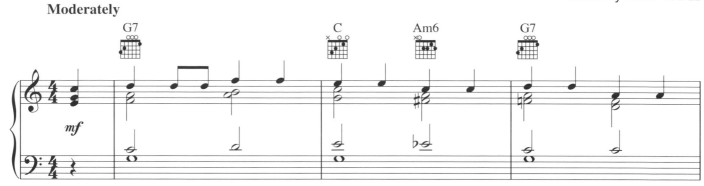

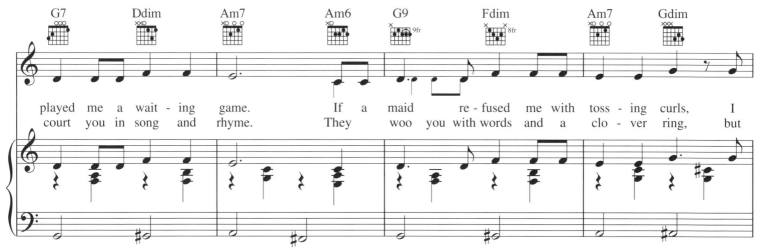

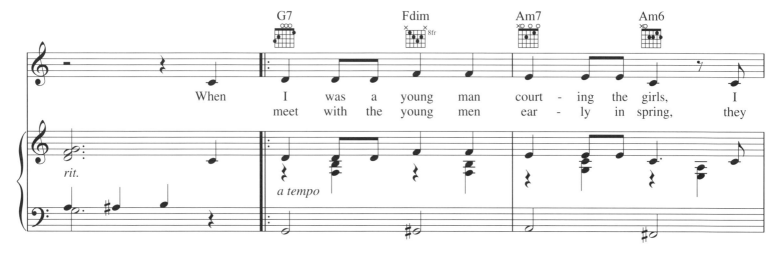

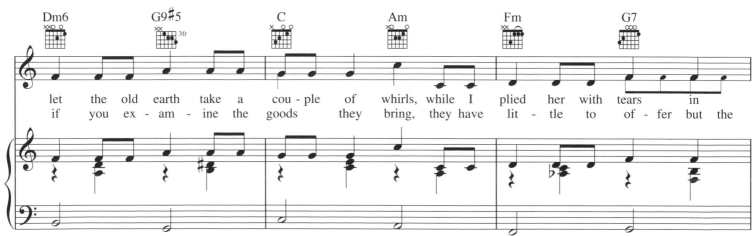

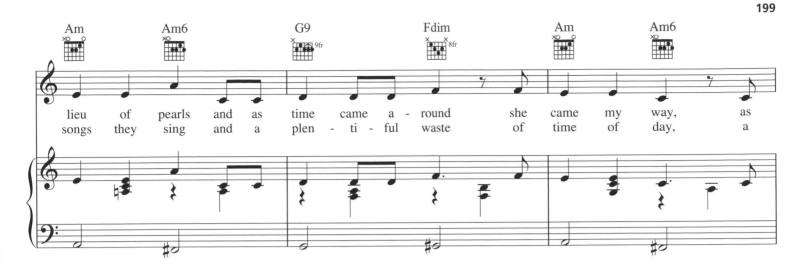

lieu of pearls and as time came a - round she came my way, as
songs they sing and a plen - ti - ful waste of time of day, a

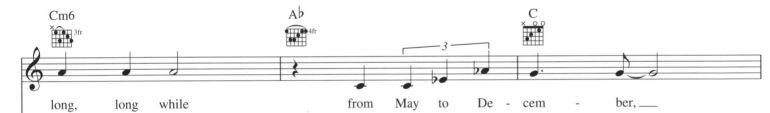

time came a - round she came.
plen - ti - ful waste of time. Oh, it's a

long, long while from May to De - cem - ber,___

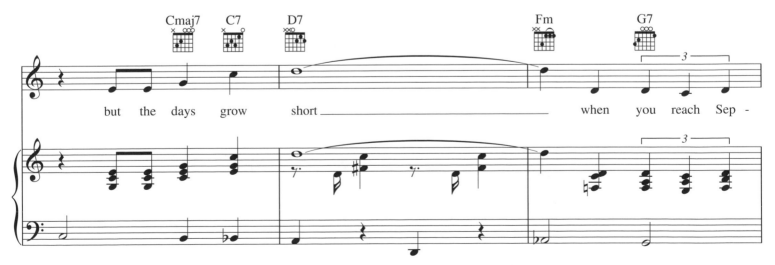

but the days grow short _____ when you reach Sep -

tem - ber. ___ When the au - tumn weath - er ___

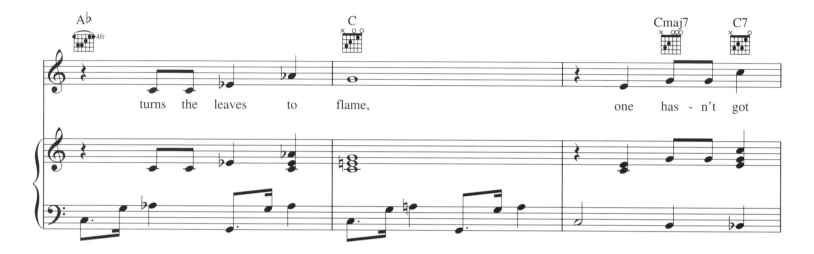

turns the leaves to flame, one has - n't got

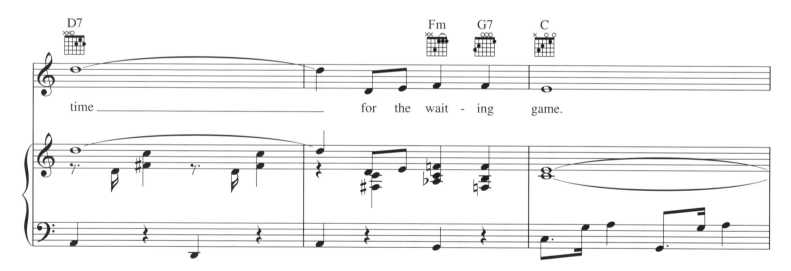

time _____ for the wait - ing game.

Oh, the days dwin - dle down ___ to a

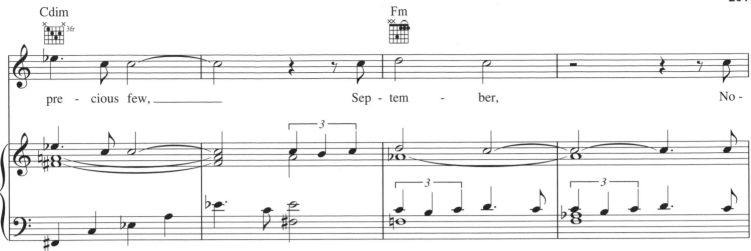

pre - cious few, _____ Sep - tem - ber, No -

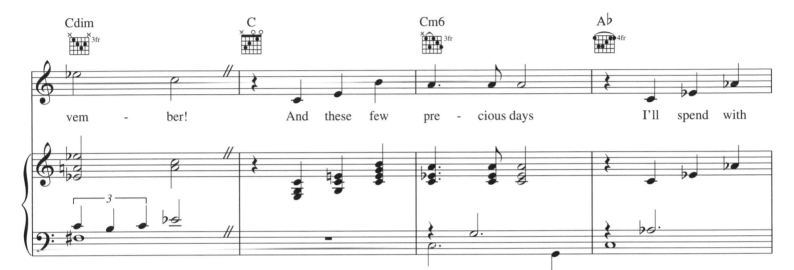

vem - ber! And these few pre - cious days I'll spend with

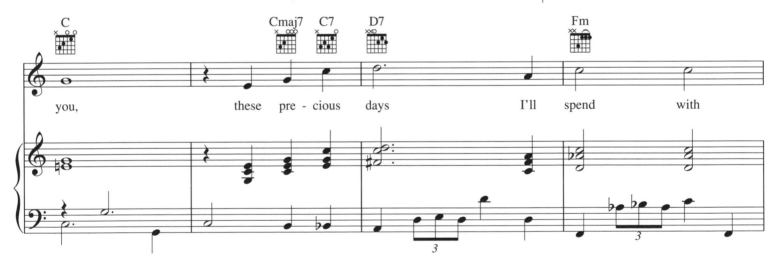

you, these pre - cious days I'll spend with

you. When you you. _____

SOME ENCHANTED EVENING

from SOUTH PACIFIC

Lyrics by OSCAR HAMMERSTEIN II
Music by RICHARD RODGERS

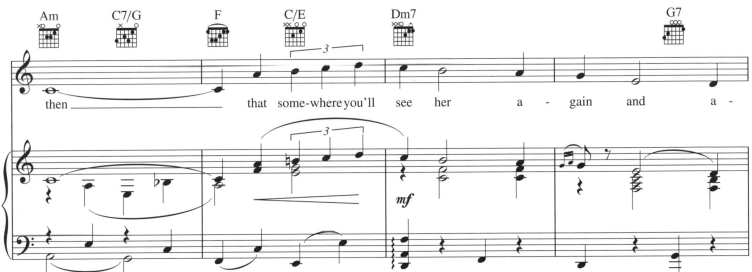

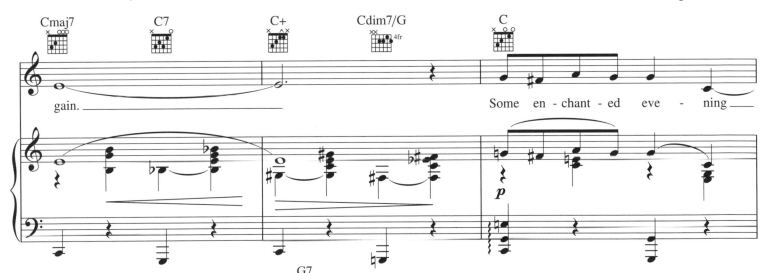

you may hear her laugh - ing ____ a - cross a crowd - ed room.

And night af - ter night, _____ as strange as it seems, ____

the sound of her laugh - ter will sing in your dreams. ____

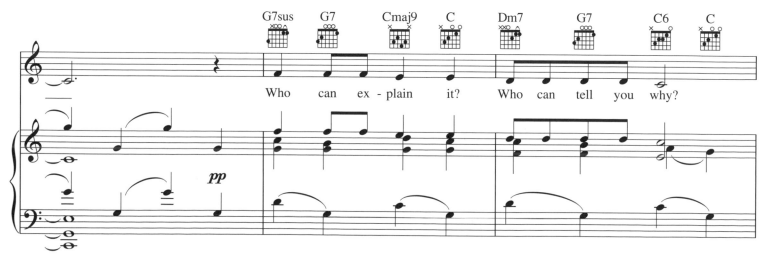

Who can ex - plain it? Who can tell you why?

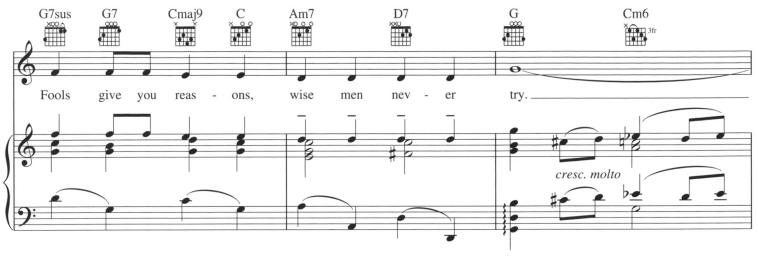

Fools give you reas - ons, wise men nev - er try. ___

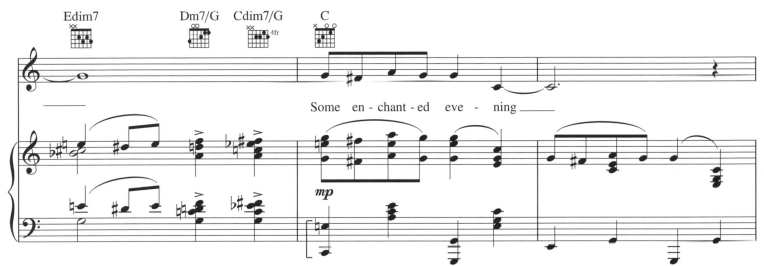

___ Some en - chant - ed eve - ning ___

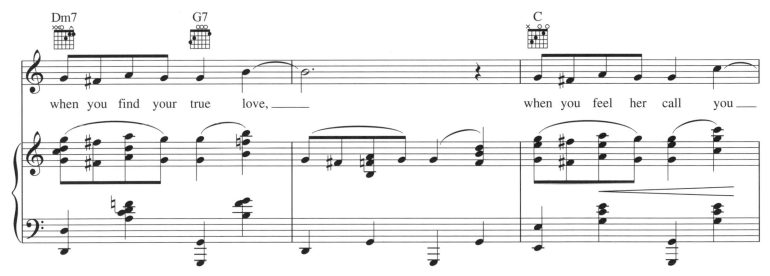

when you find your true love, ___ when you feel her call you ___

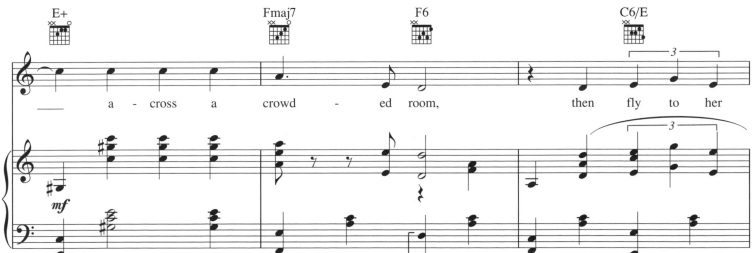

___ a - cross a crowd - ed room, then fly to her

side _____ and make her your own, _____ or all through your

life you may dream all a - lone. _____

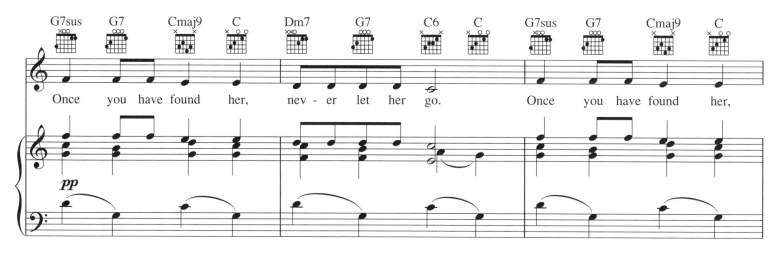

Once you have found her, nev - er let her go. Once you have found her,

Nev - er let her go! _____

THERE'S A SMALL HOTEL

from ON YOUR TOES

Words by LORENZ HART
Music by RICHARD RODGERS

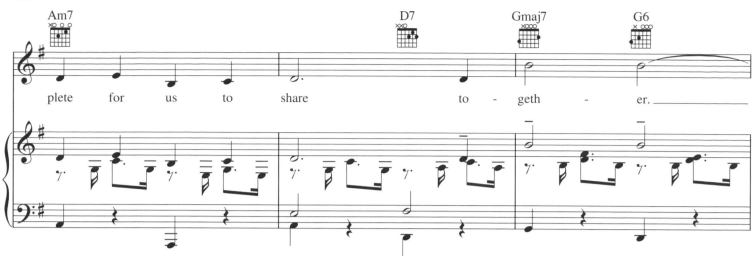

plete for us to share to - geth - er. ____

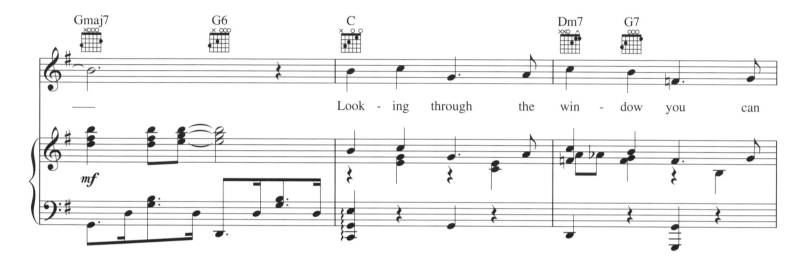

____ Look - ing through the win - dow you can

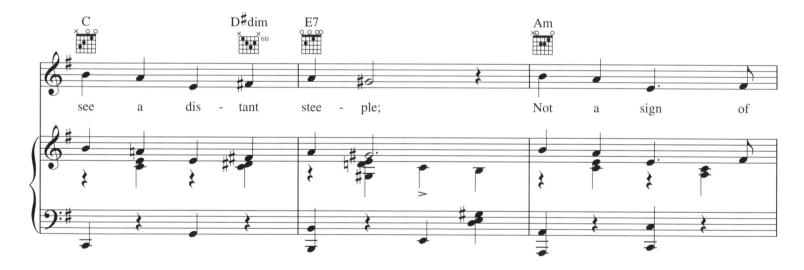

see a dis - tant stee - ple; Not a sign of

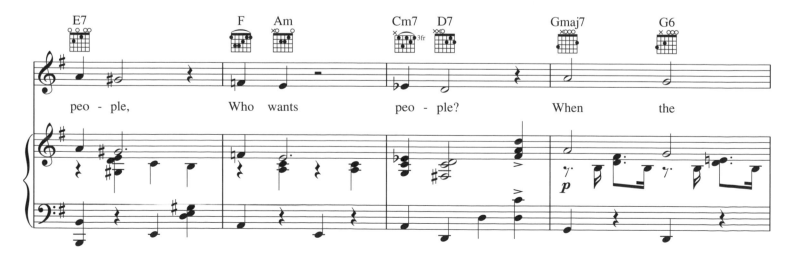

peo - ple, Who wants peo - ple? When the

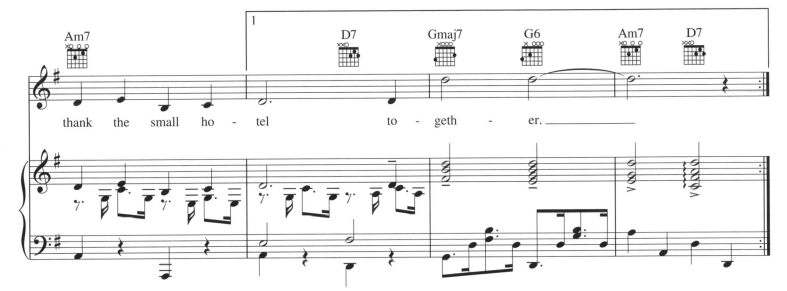

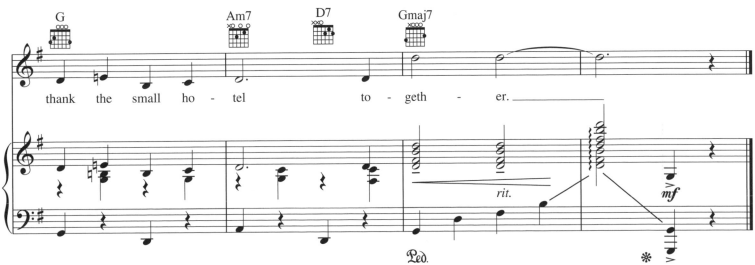

STRANGER IN PARADISE

from KISMET

Words and Music by ROBERT WRIGHT
and GEORGE FORREST
(Music based on Themes of A. BORODIN)

211

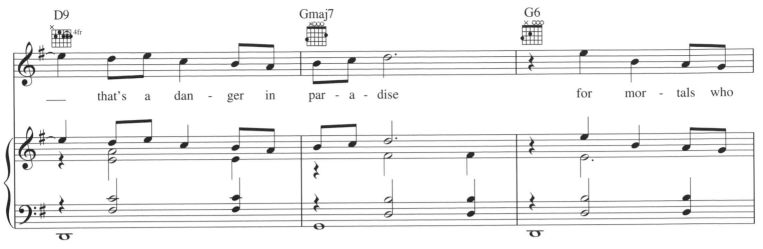

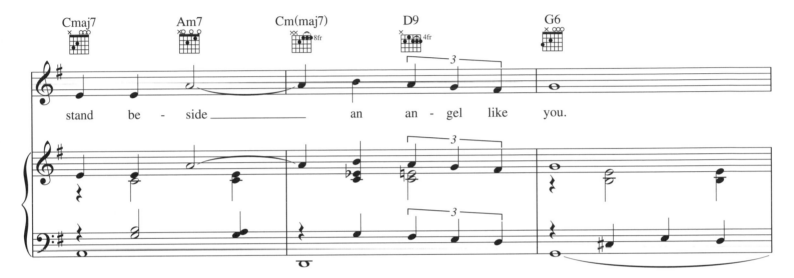

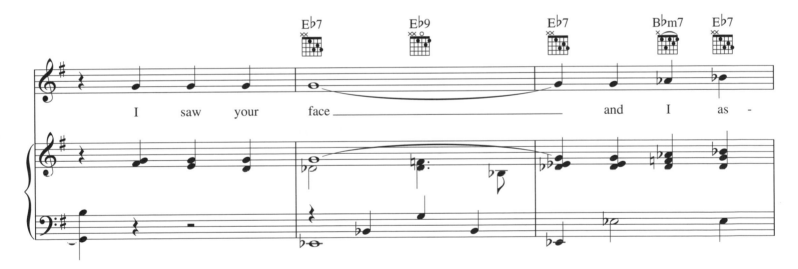

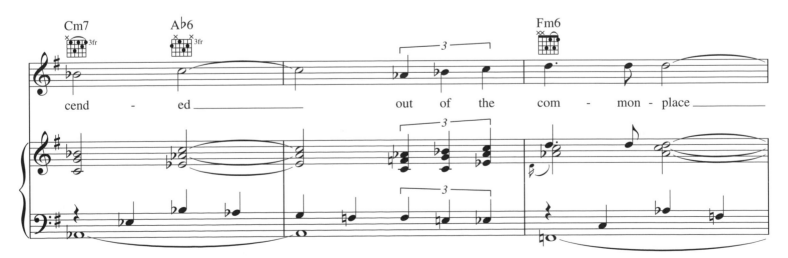

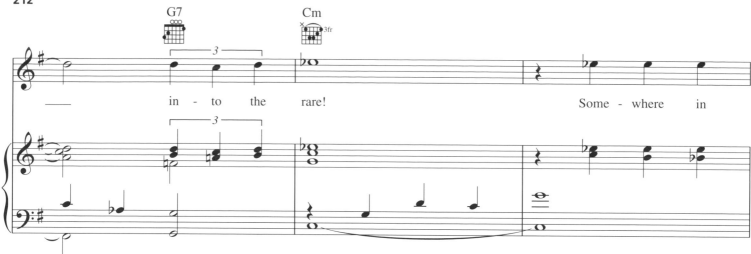

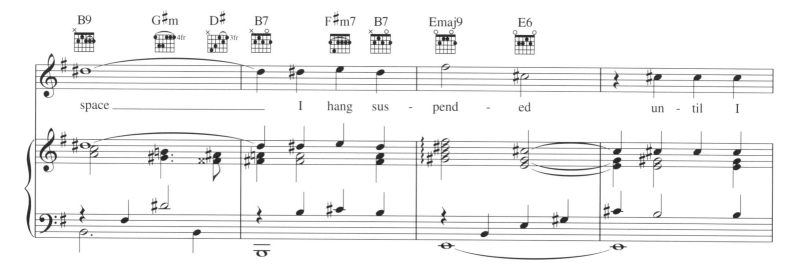

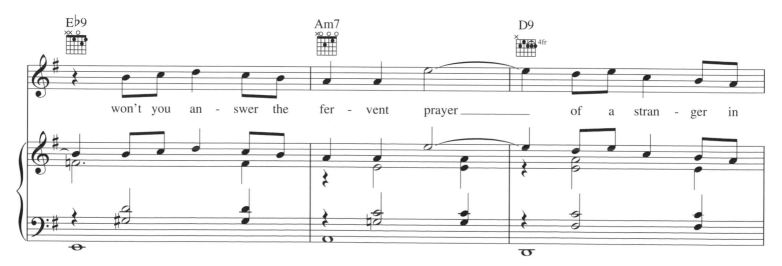

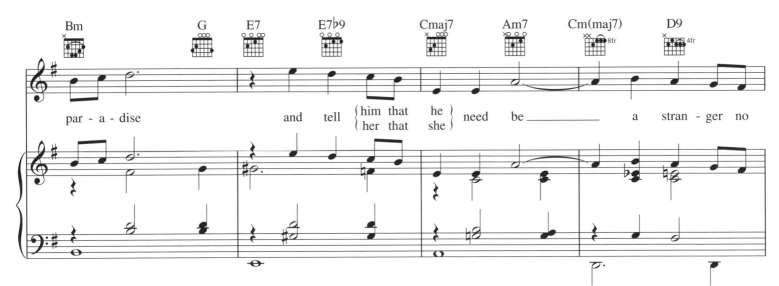

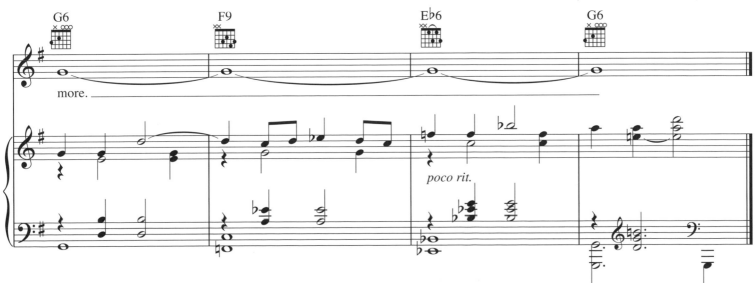

SUNRISE, SUNSET
from the Musical FIDDLER ON THE ROOF

Words by SHELDON HARNICK
Music by JERRY BOCK

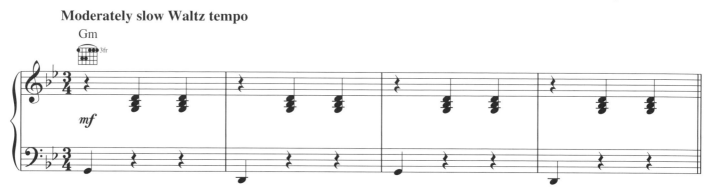

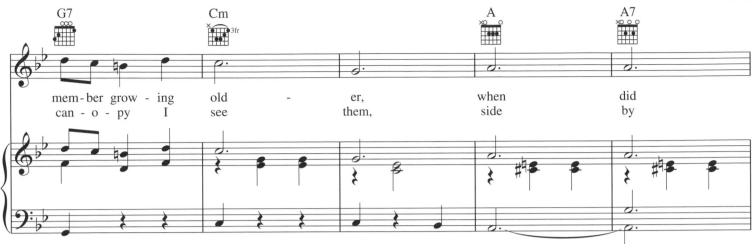

mem-ber grow - ing old - - er, when did
can - o - py I see them, side by

they? _____
side. _____

When did she get to be a beau -
Place the gold ring a-round her fin -

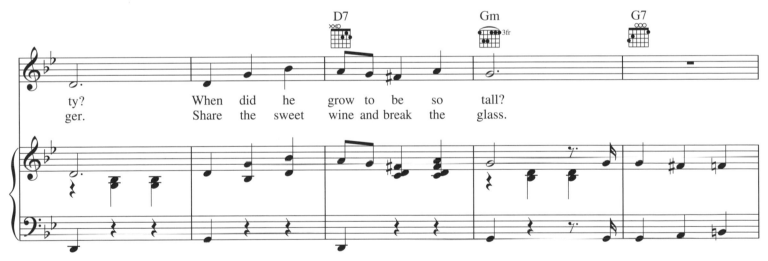

ty? When did he grow to be so tall?
ger. Share the sweet wine and break the glass.

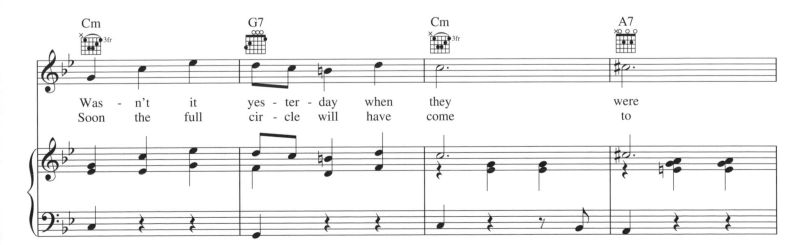

Was - n't it yes - ter - day when they were
Soon the full cir - cle will have come to

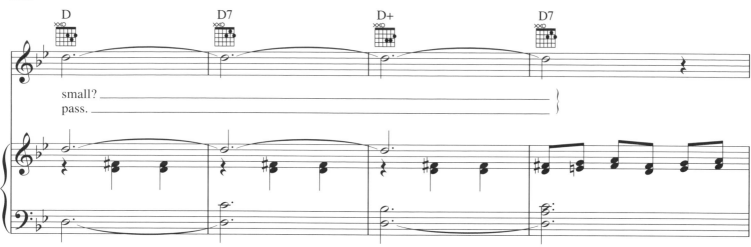

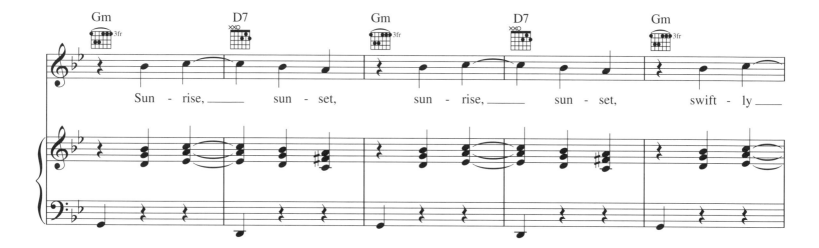

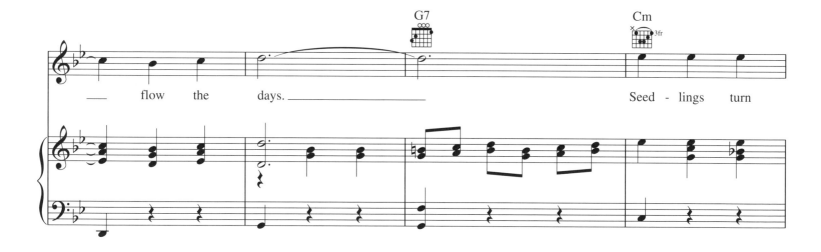

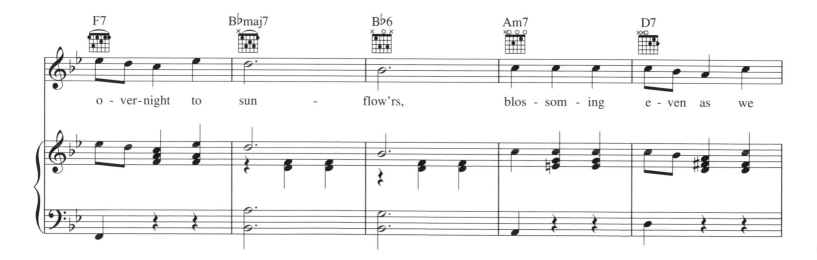

gaze. _____ Sun - rise, _____ sun - set, sun - rise, _

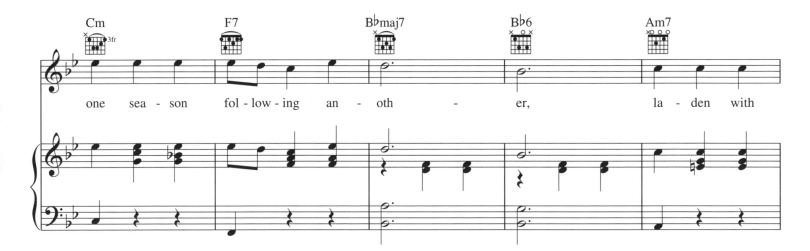

_ sun - set, swift - ly _____ fly the years; _____

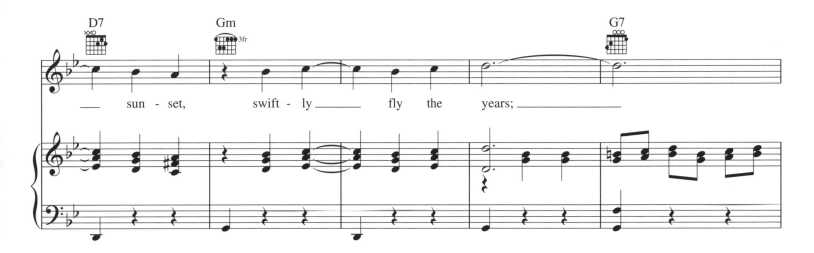

one sea - son fol - low - ing an - oth - er, la - den with

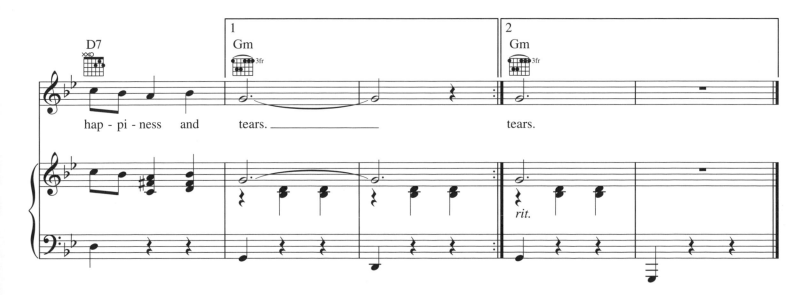

hap - pi - ness and tears. _____ tears.

'TIL HIM
from THE PRODUCERS

Music and Lyrics by
MEL BROOKS

Moderate Ballad

LEO:
No one ev-er made me feel like some-one 'til him.

Life was real-ly noth-ing but a glum one 'til him.

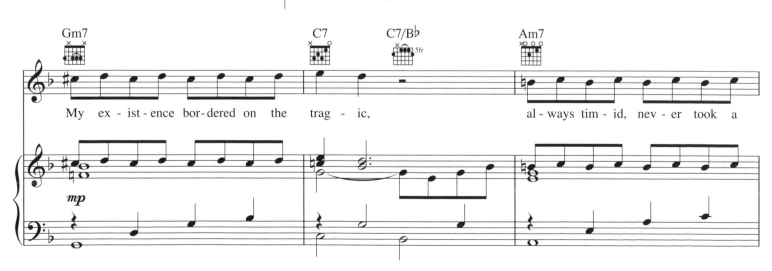

My ex-ist-ence bor-dered on the trag-ic,   al-ways tim-id, nev-er took a

219

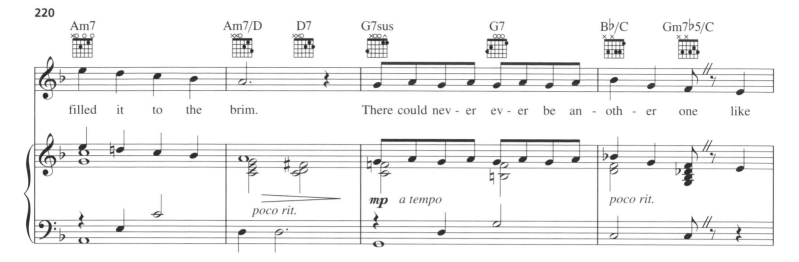

filled it to the brim. There could nev-er ev-er be an-oth-er one like

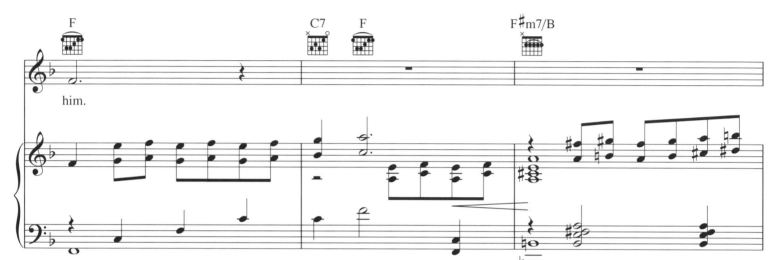

him.

MAX: No one ev-er ev-er real-ly knew me 'til

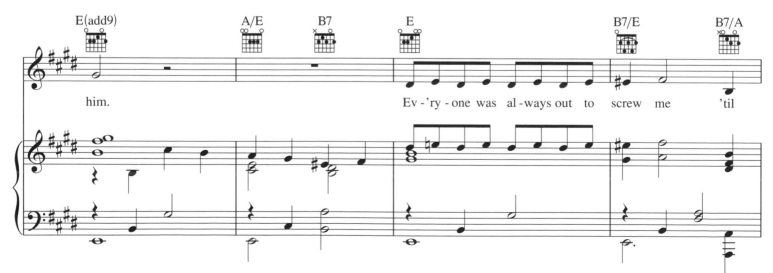

him. Ev-'ry-one was al-ways out to screw me 'til

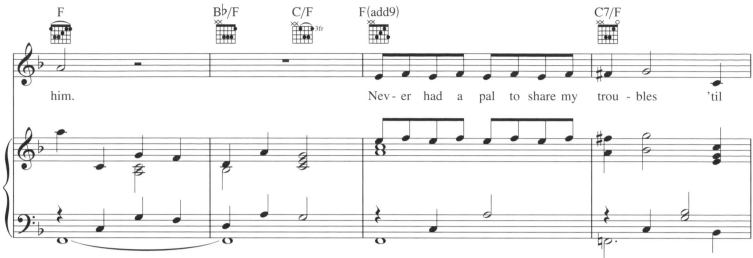

him.

Nev - er had a pal to share my trou - bles 'til

him.

LEO & MAX: He filled up my emp - ty life,

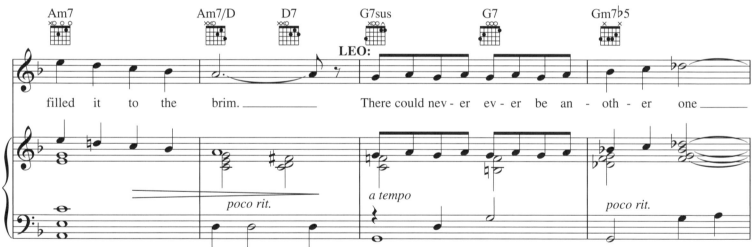

filled it to the brim. _____ **LEO:** There could nev - er ev - er be an - oth - er one _____

poco rit. *a tempo* *poco rit.*

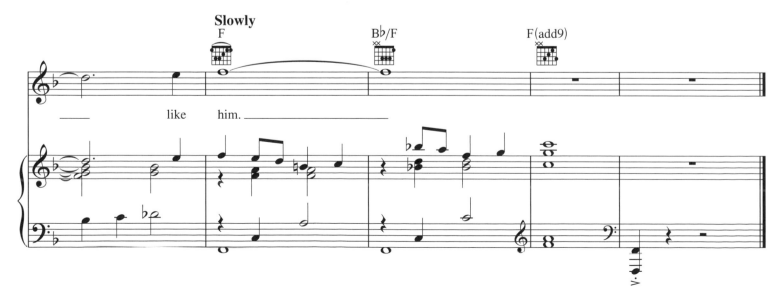

Slowly

_____ like him. _____

TILL THERE WAS YOU
from Meredith Willson's THE MUSIC MAN

By MEREDITH WILLSON

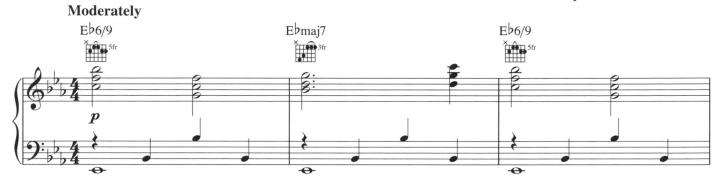

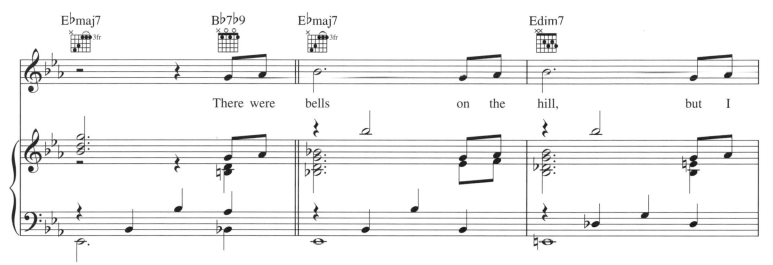

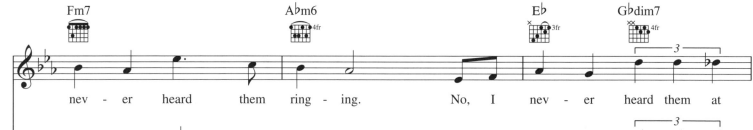

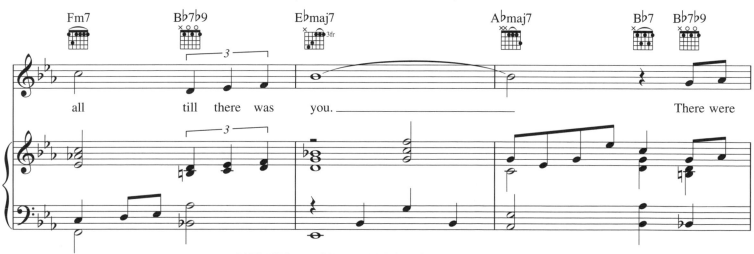

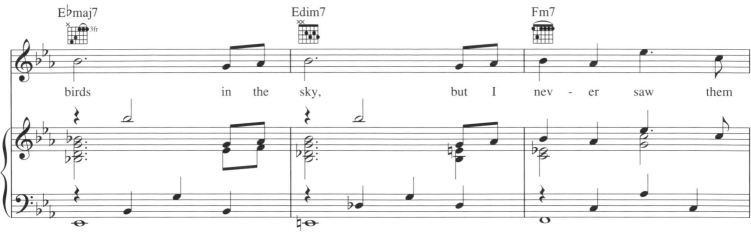

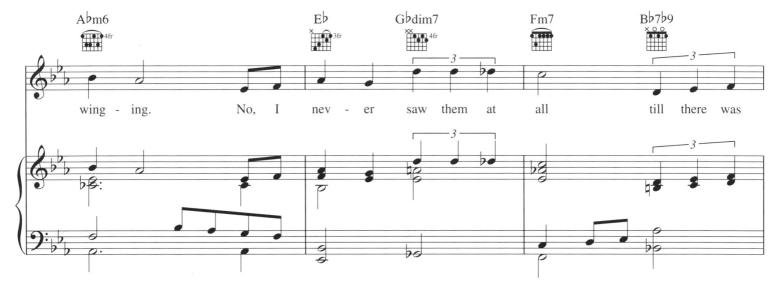

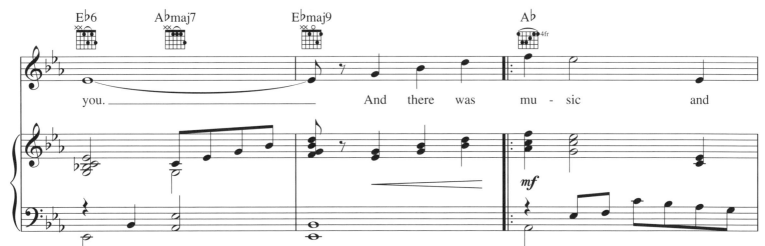

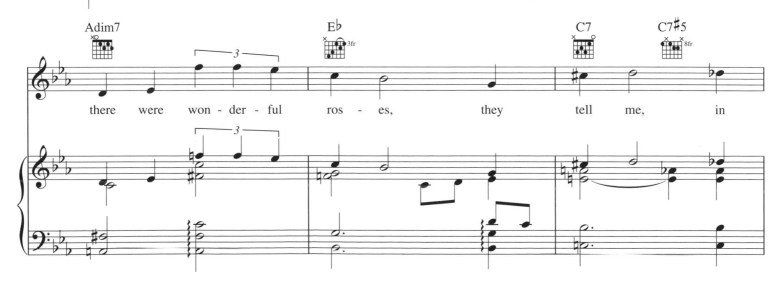

TOMORROW
from the Musical Production ANNIE

Lyric by MARTIN CHARNIN
Music by CHARLES STROUSE

Moderately slow

The sun - 'll come out _____ to - mor - row,
bet your bot - tom dol - lar that to - mor - row _____ there'll be
sun! Jus' think - ing a - bout _____ to - mor - row

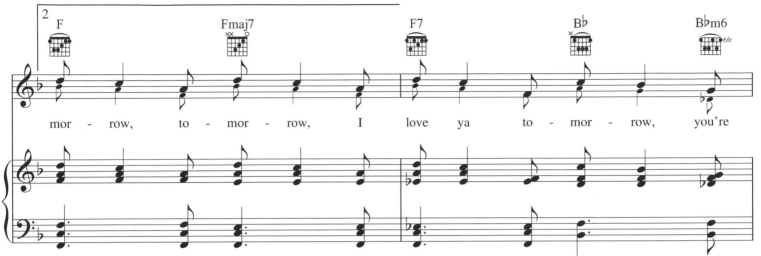

mor - row, to - mor - row, I love ya to - mor - row, you're

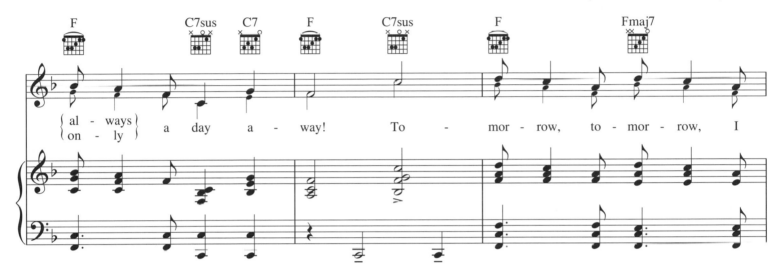

{al - ways}
{on - ly} a day a - way! To - mor - row, to - mor - row, I

love ya to - mor - row, you're {al - ways}{on - ly} a day a -

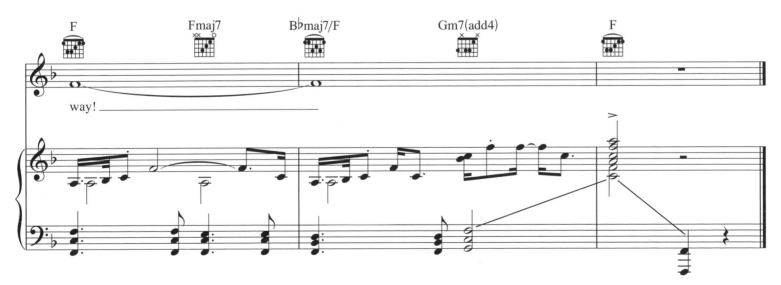

way! _____

WHAT I DID FOR LOVE
from A CHORUS LINE

Music by MARVIN HAMLISCH
Lyric by EDWARD KLEBAN

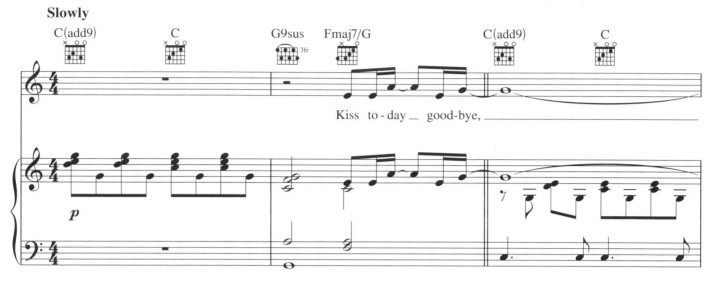

what I did for love, ___ what I did for love. ___

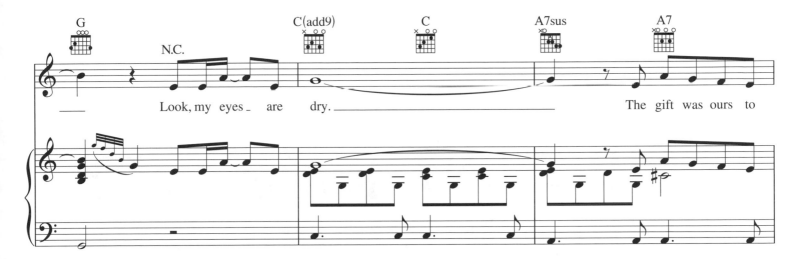

___ Look, my eyes ___ are dry. ___ The gift was ours to

bor - row. ___ It's as if ___ we al - ways

knew. ___ And I won't for-get ___ what I did for love, ___

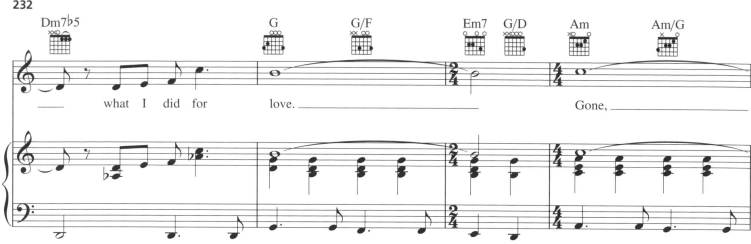

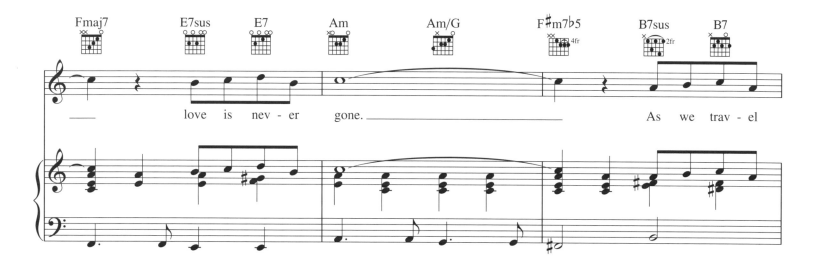

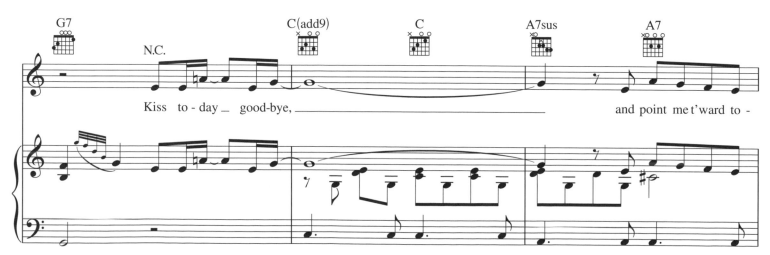

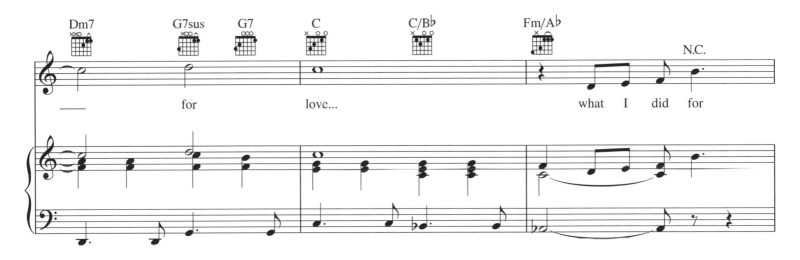

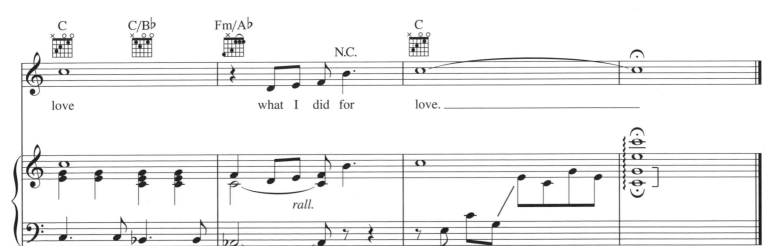

WHO CAN I TURN TO
(When Nobody Needs Me)
from THE ROAR OF THE GREASEPAINT – THE SMELL OF THE CROWD

Words and Music by LESLIE BRICUSSE
and ANTHONY NEWLEY

Slowly, with expression

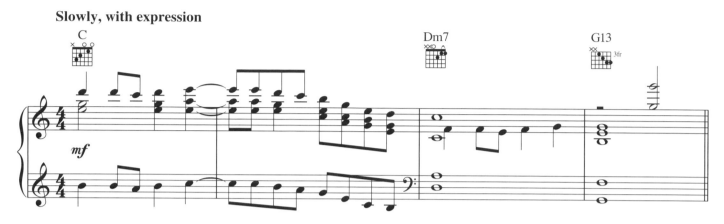

Who can I turn to _____ when no-bod-y needs me? _____ My

heart wants to know and so I must go where des-ti-ny leads me. _____

235

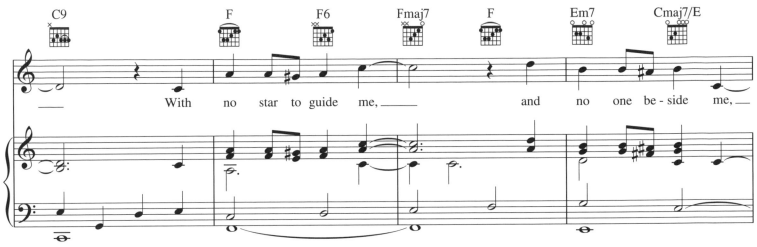

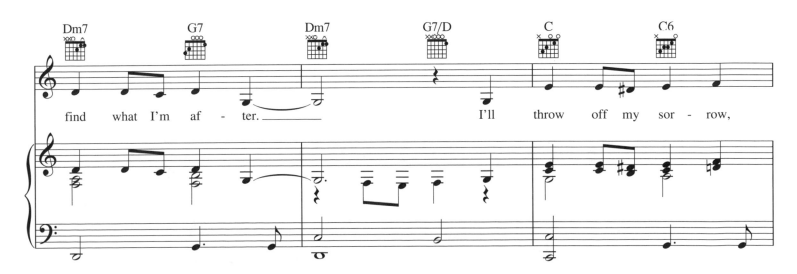

236

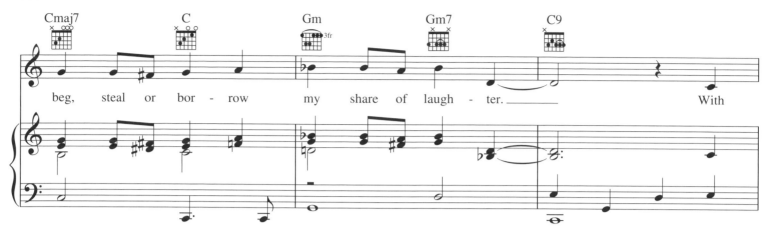

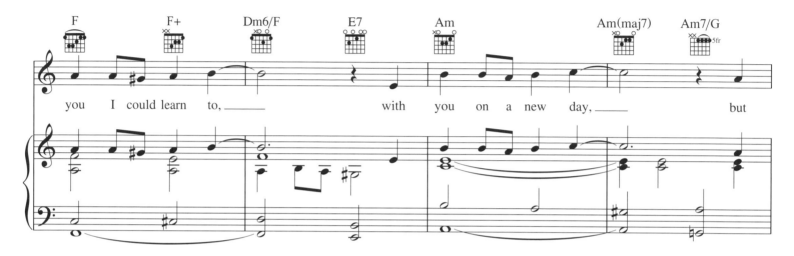

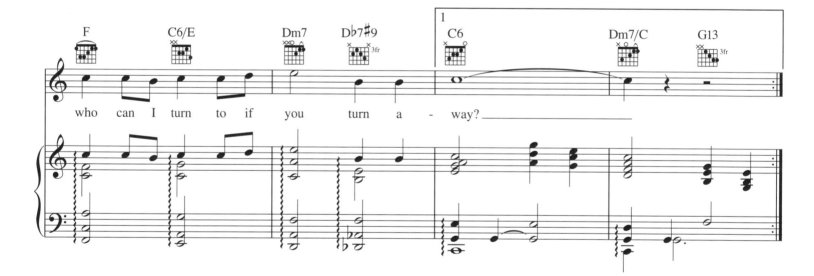

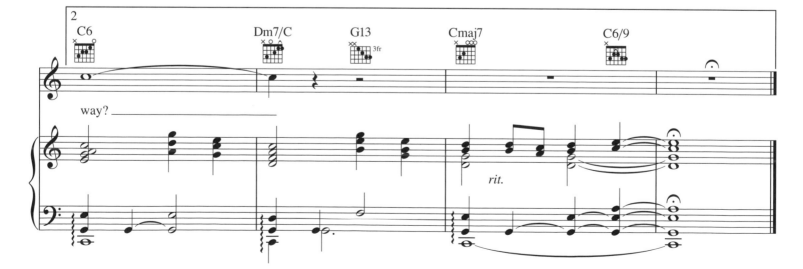

YOU'LL NEVER WALK ALONE

from CAROUSEL

Lyrics by OSCAR HAMMERSTEIN II
Music by RICHARD RODGERS

Andantino molto cantabile

(with great warmth, like a hymn)

* alternate lyric: hold your head up high

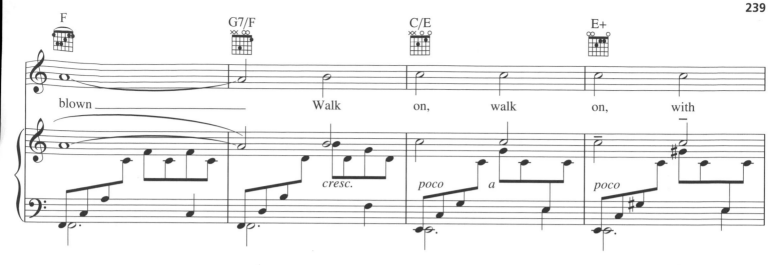

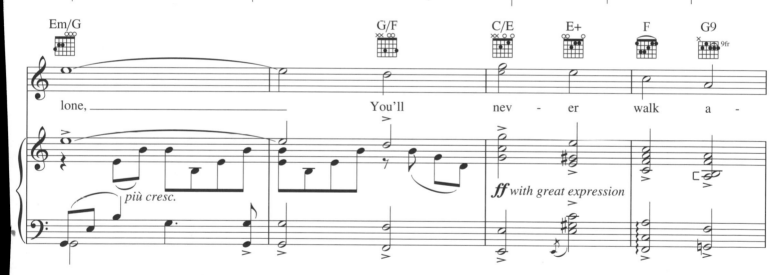

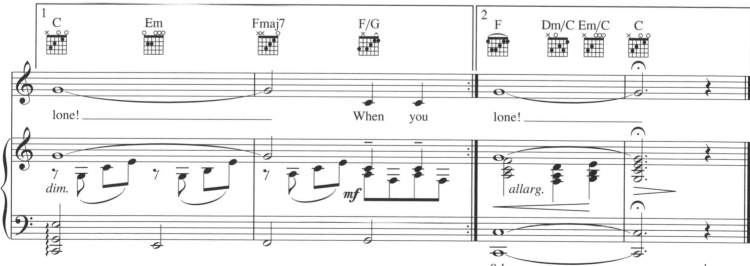

HAL LEONARD:
Your Source for the Best of Broadway

THE BEST BROADWAY SONGS EVER

Over 70 songs from Broadway's latest and greatest hit shows: As Long as He Needs Me • Bess, You Is My Woman • Bewitched • Comedy Tonight • Don't Cry for Me Argentina • Getting to Know You • I Could Have Danced All Night • I Dreamed a Dream • If I Were a Rich Man • The Last Night of the World • Love Changes Everything • Oklahoma • Ol' Man River • People • Try to Remember • and more.

00309155 Piano/Vocal/Guitar..................................$24.95

THE BIG BOOK OF BROADWAY

This edition includes 70 songs from classic musicals and recent blockbusters like *The Producers, Aida* and *Hairspray*. Includes: Bring Him Home • Camelot • Everything's Coming Up Roses • The Impossible Dream • A Lot of Livin' to Do • One • Some Enchanted Evening • Thoroughly Modern Millie • Till There Was You • and more.

00311658 Piano/Vocal/Guitar $19.95

BROADWAY CLASSICS

PIANO PLAY-ALONG SERIES, VOLUME 4
This book/CD pack provides keyboardists with a full performance track and a separate backing track for each tune. Songs include: Ain't Misbehavin' • Cabaret • If I Were a Bell • Memory • Oklahoma • Some Enchanted Evening • The Sound of Music • You'll Never Walk Alone.

00311075 Book/CD Pack $14.95

BROADWAY DELUXE

125 of Broadway's biggest show tunes! Includes such showstoppers as: Bewitched • Cabaret • Camelot • Day by Day • Hello Young Lovers • I Could Have Danced All Night • I Talk to the Trees • I've Grown Accustomed to Her Face • If Ever I Would Leave You • The Lady Is a Tramp • My Heart Belongs to Daddy • Oklahoma • September Song • Seventy Six Trombones • Try to Remember • and more!

00309245 Piano/Vocal/Guitar $24.95

BROADWAY SONGS

Get more bang for your buck with this jam-packed collection of 73 songs from 56 shows, including *Annie Get Your Gun, Cabaret, The Full Monty, Jekyll & Hyde, Les Misérables, Oklahoma* and more. Songs: Any Dream Will Do • Consider Yourself • Footloose • Getting to Know You • I Dreamed a Dream • One • People • Summer Nights • The Surrey with the Fringe on Top • With One Look • and more.

00310832 Piano/Vocal/Guitar..................................$12.95

CONTEMPORARY BROADWAY

44 songs from 25 contemporary musicals and Broadway revivals. Includes: And All That Jazz (*Chicago*) • Dancing Queen (*Mamma Mia!*) • Good Morning Baltimore (*Hairspray*) • Mein Herr (*Cabaret*) • Popular (*Wicked*) • Purpose (*Avenue Q*) • Seasons of Love (*Rent*) • When You Got It, Flaunt It (*The Producers*) • You Rule My World (*The Full Monty*) • and more.

00310796 Piano/Vocal/Guitar..................................$18.95

DEFINITIVE BROADWAY

142 of the greatest show tunes ever, including: Don't Cry for Me Argentina • Hello, Dolly! • I Dreamed a Dream • Lullaby of Broadway • Mack the Knife • Memory • Send in the Clowns • Somewhere • The Sound of Music • Strike Up the Band • Summertime • Sunrise, Sunset • Tea for Two • Tomorrow • What I Did for Love • and more.

00359570 Piano/Vocal/Guitar..................................$24.95

ESSENTIAL SONGS: BROADWAY

Over 100 songs are included in this top-notch collection: Any Dream Will Do • Blue Skies • Cabaret • Don't Cry for Me, Argentina • Edelweiss • Hello, Dolly! • I'll Be Seeing You • Memory • The Music of the Night • Oklahoma • Seasons of Love • Summer Nights • There's No Business like Show Business • Tomorrow • and more.

00311222 Piano/Vocal/Guitar $24.95

KIDS' BROADWAY SONGBOOK

An unprecedented collection of songs originally performed by children on the Broadway stage. Includes 16 songs for boys and girls, including: Gary, Indiana (*The Music Man*) • Castle on a Cloud (*Les Misérables*) • Where Is Love? (*Oliver!*) • Tomorrow (*Annie*) • and more.

00311609 Book Only.....................................$14.95
00740149 Book/CD Pack...............................$22.95

THE OFF-BROADWAY SONGBOOK

42 gems from off-Broadway hits, including *Godspell, Tick Tick...Boom!, The Fantasticks, Once upon a Mattress, The Wild Party* and more. Songs include: Always a Bridesmaid • Come to Your Senses • Day by Day • Happiness • How Glory Goes • I Hate Musicals • The Picture in the Hall • Soon It's Gonna Rain • Stars and the Moon • Still Hurting • Twilight • and more.

00311168 Piano/Vocal/Guitar $16.95

THE TONY AWARDS SONGBOOK

This collection assembles songs from each of Tony-winning Best Musicals through "Mama Who Bore Me" from 2007 winner *Spring Awakening*. Songs include: Til There Was You • The Sound of Music • Hello, Dolly! • Sunrise, Sunset • Send in the Clowns • Tomorrow • Memory • I Dreamed a Dream • Seasons of Love • Circle of Life • Mama, I'm a Big Girl Now • and more. Includes photos and a table of contents listed both chronologically and alphabetically.

00311092 Piano/Vocal/Guitar $19.95

THE ULTIMATE BROADWAY FAKE BOOK

Over 700 songs from more than 200 Broadway shows! Songs include: All I Ask of You • Bewitched • Cabaret • Don't Cry for Me Argentina • Edelweiss • Getting to Know You • Hello, Dolly! • If I Were a Rich Man • Last Night of the World • The Music of the Night • Oklahoma • People • Seasons of Love • Tell Me on a Sunday • Unexpected Song • and more!

00240046 Melody/Lyrics/Chords....................$45.00

ULTIMATE BROADWAY PLATINUM

100 popular Broadway songs: As If We Never Said Goodbye • Bye Bye Birdie • Camelot • Everything's Coming Up Roses • Gigi • Hello, Young Lovers • I Enjoy Being a Girl • Just in Time • My Favorite Things • On a Clear Day • People • Sun and Moon • Try to Remember • Who Can I Turn To • Younger Than Springtime • and many more.

00311496 Piano/Vocal/Guitar $19.95

Prices, contents, and availability subject to change without notice.
Some products may not be available outside the U.S.A.

FOR MORE INFORMATION, SEE YOUR LOCAL MUSIC DEALER,
OR WRITE TO:

HAL•LEONARD®
CORPORATION
7777 W. BLUEMOUND RD. P.O. BOX 13819 MILWAUKEE, WI 53213

Get complete songlists and more at www.halleonard.com   0308